The Best of CLASSROOM CLANGERS

Selected and Compiled by

John G Muir

Illustrated by George J Glass

GORDON WRIGHT PUBLISHING
25 MAYFIELD ROAD, EDINBURGH EH9 2NQ
SCOTLAND

British Library Cataloguing in Publication Data
A Catalogue for this book is
available from the British Library.

ISBN 0 903065 84 3

Cover illustration: George J Glass.
Cover design: John Haxby.

Typeset by Gordon Wright Publishing Ltd., Edinburgh.
Printed and Bound by Redwood Books, Trowbridge, Wiltshire.

The Best of Classroom Clangers

by the Same Author

Classroom Clangers	Gordon Wright Publishing (1984)
More Classroom Clangers	Gordon Wright Publishing (1986)
Even More Classroom Clangers	Mainstream Publishing (1989)
More Than my Job's Worth	Christian Focus Publications (1993)
Divided Loyalties Shared Beliefs	Christian Focus Publications (1994)
An Inspector Recalls	Scottish Cultural Press (1995)

Contents

To
Gwen, Valerie and Lesley

Foreword

It is over ten years since I put together the first collection of *Classroom Clangers*. The resulting publicity took me and my publisher by surprise and the first print run sold out within a couple of weeks. For the next few years teachers from all over the country sent me favourite howlers which they had written down and a further two selections hit the bookstands in quick succession.

There is still demand for them it seems, the unconscious humour of children as popular as ever, so it was proposed that I should put together a selection of those which have raised the most laughs and add a few new ones. More than ever these days teachers, snowed under with demands from all quarters, survive by maintaining a lively sense of humour. I hope that this bumper edition of *The Best of Classroom Clangers* will keep them laughing.

John G Muir

18

A Teacher's Lot . . .

Is rarely a happy one.

Drives a man to drink, golf, or insanity.

A thirty-nine hour week stretched to seventy and beyond.

A professional who demeans his or her status to that of a labourer.

A cross between a nurse and a policeman.

In *Loco Parentis* but devoid of parental support.

For men who cannot find labouring jobs to suit their state of health.

Someone for children to vent their disrespect on.

Life expectancy: three years after retirement.

* * * * * *

If she doesn't get married she'll have to stay in teaching all her life.

My daddy's not a gentleman, he's a teacher.

Poor man, even when he gets married he has to stick at that job.

She's just a young lassie but she'll probably be all right if she stays an infant teacher.

You should take up teaching; it's a nice easy job with grand holidays.

She's only got an infant class just now, but if she does well they'll probably put her further up.

He's not really a teacher, he takes P.E.

Telling Tales

The teacher was rather puzzled when one of her pupils came to school regularly with a lot of biscuits which he distributed among his friends. She thought she would ask him where he got them, but he refused at first to tell her. Thinking that he may be up to some mischief she took him aside and insisted that he tell her. 'Please Miss, my mum works in the biscuit factory and she smuggles them out in her knickers . . .' he blurted out to the shocked teacher.

Having successfully quietened the group of children in the dining room, the headmaster folded his arms and calmly said, 'Now, you will all sit there and eat your lunch without opening your mouths.'

'Please Sir, what did you write at the foot of my page?' 'Can't you read boy, it says "your writing is illegible".'

From a secondary school handbook, an unfortunate example of the school's discipline referral system.
'When a pupil is referred by an assistant teacher for refusal to carry out a punishment exercise, that pupil should be warned by the Principal Teacher and suspended in that teacher's room for the rest of the day . . .'

A youngster spilt milk on his trousers one morning and leapt to his feet shouting 'Good God, look what I've done!' The young teacher was horrified and sent him to the headmaster to report he had used bad language. He arrived at the headmaster's study, knocked quietly and was admitted. 'Please Sir, Miss Nichols has sent me here for using bad language.' 'Good God boy!' said the headmaster, 'What on earth did you say?'

The boys' school was to become co-educational after the holidays with a first influx of girl pupils. The lads were quite excited and one arrived home to report to his parents, 'Guess what? After the holidays the school's becoming bisexual.'

Ann, a red-haired 'hard nut' in an upper secondary school arrived in class having obviously been recently involved in a fight. The teacher, 'concerned' for her welfare, enquired as to the reasons for the fracas and learned that she had been involved in a fight with another girl. Ann admitted that she had started the fight but was reluctant to tell why. After some persuasion she confessed, in a broad Scottish accent, 'She called me a bad name, Sur. I cannae tell ye whit it wis, but it starts wi an H.'

In another incident the same Ann was stopped in the corridor, apparently skipping a class. When asked where she thought she was going, she replied casually, 'Ah'm suppost tae be at Sex wi Mr Sutherland but ah cannae find him.'

When a teacher introduced work cards to her class she was amused to learn from a parent one evening that her son had gone home and told her, 'We played card games for most of the afternoon.'

A parent was intrigued when her little daughter said that her teacher was wearing a wig. 'How do you know it's a wig?' she asked.
'Of course it is, I see her putting it on every day.'
The situation was clarified when the mother saw the teacher walking down the road from school wearing a fur hat!

Every infant teacher keeps spare clothes in school for the little 'accidents' which occur from time to time. One little girl wet herself and the teacher discreetly changed her and sent the soiled pants home in a carrier bag. Next day, travelling on the bus with her father, the little girl noticed her teacher in the seat in front of her and in a loud voice said, 'Mrs MacFarlane, my daddy's got yer knickers in his pocket.'

A pupil in a class made a rude remark under his breath but would not own up. The teacher threatened to punish the whole class if the person did not stand up immediately. He spoke to each one in turn but nobody confessed so he began to punish everyone. When he came to the last one he was both exhausted and exasperated and said, 'Now if you tell me who did it I'll let you off, but if you don't you will get more than anyone else.'
'Okay, Sir,' came the quick response, 'I did it.'

Having reprimanded a boy for showing off pages from a girlie magazine, which the pupil said he had found in the school waste-paper bin, the headmaster thought he had better make an announcement. 'Now, if anyone finds anything like that again, they must show it to me first.'

Noticeboard

Will staff please note that the large space at the front of the building is reserved for the Headmaster.

If you think you have a problem you should see the head teacher.

It is easy to electrocute yourself with this equipment. You must ask the teacher how to do it.

If you find any big drips in your classroom this morning please report them to the janitor.

The Keep Fit Club will be held in the gym at lunch time each Monday. Mr. Leadbetter is looking for another member of staff to support him.

Any chemicals in the lab. cupboard marked 'poison' must only be given to members of staff.

Anybody who speaks French could teach it to a class of 14-year-olds.

First offenders must always be suspended by the head.

The headmaster should send the names of all staff, broken down by sex and age, to the Education Office.

As the football pitch is water-logged, class 4a will do swimming instead.

Please note that all pupils not present must be marked absent.

Any pupil wishing to take part in throwing the discus can practise with Mr Smith any afternoon this week.

Nursery School Circular: Please return any underwear borrowed from the headteacher as she may need it in case of 'emergencies'.

If you are looking for the janitor, he can be found dealing with a problem in the girls' toilets.

The infant staff are collecting toilet rolls. Please pass on used ones to them.

Found on the floor of a staff room: Please replace drawing pins borrowed from this notice board.

School Canteen Notice: DESERT: CHOCOLATE MOUSE.

Dear Teacher

The average parent is an adept apologist as these extracts from notes indicate:

Please excuse Jane for being absent from school. She had an ulster in her throat.

Please excuse Mary for being absent. She will be absent a long time. The doctor says she has an absent in the brain.

Please excuse Jenny's absence. She came home on Tuesday afternoon with it and we just can't get rid of it.

Please excuse Moira for not being at school this week. I have been upside down with the painters for the last three days.

John has been in bed for two days with his head.

Although Susan left in good time she had to come back home with her stomach.

I kept Jean at home yesterday because my wife had twins but I can assure you that this will not happen again.

Dear Sir, Tommy is absent because of his face, he has had it a long time and the doctor says it is spreading.

Please excuse Jacqueline for being off school yesterday. She was hanging on to the mantlepiece with her stomach.

Jamie did not attend school yesterday because he was evaporated with constipation.

Lizzie was very bad with pans in her tummy.

Dear Sir, please excuse James from being late as I slept in the smorning.

Sorry John is off but he has information of the lungs, with combinations.

I have been in bed for three days with the doctor and couldn't get up to get him dressed.

Dear Sir, thanks for all you have done for our James. May God guard and keep you from Mrs Brown.

Dear Sir, please excuse Sebastian for being absent from school as he had diahero.

Please excuse Mary being absent from school as I had to go to bed and oblige.
Yours truly,
Mrs Watson.

The class teacher was very concerned about one little boy in her room whose personal hygiene left a lot to be desired, so she wrote a very tactful letter to the mother suggesting that regular baths might solve the problem. Back came the reply: Dear Teacher, There is no problem. It is your job to teach, not to smell!

Please excuse Bobby for being late. We had a very big dinner today.

Please excuse Mary from being absent but she was kept at home to help her mother wash yours truly her father.

I'm sorry Peggy is unable to attend school as she fell and cut her knee on a piece of glass and is now suffering from a pane in the leg.

I regret to say Walter is in bed with a chill again. I just can't get him to pass water. He insists on jumping into every puddle he sees.

Bobby was not able to come to school because he hasn't been yet. The doctor says that it would be better if he stayed at home until he goes. When he has gone I will send him back.

I am sorry George was absent from school yesterday, but he had the skitters. (Sorry I can't spell the proper word.)

Sorry Jimmy is late this morning as he hurt his neck and I overslept into the bargain.

Dear Mr Forbes, Thankyou for your letter. I am glad you admit you were wrong, which just goes to show that teachers aren't imflammable.

Pamela will take squash, she is willing to be couched on Mondays.

Pauline is late because she had toothache. I told her she would have to go to the dentist, but she seems to be alright now.

Please excuse Marion from stripping for P.E. as she has had a bit of a chill and is suffering from a touch of diarrhoea. Would it be alright if she did it in her tracksuit?

Jim could not come to school this morning as he spent most of the night vomiting up the shepherd's pie and trifle he had for his supper. I think he must have caught a virus.

I would like my son to have a real vacation like teaching.

Parent: Why is my daughter's mark for French so low?
Teacher: She has been a bit lazy recently so we thought we would give her a fright.
Parent: What are you running here, a French department or a blooming ghost train?

Susan did not come back to school after lunch because her dad turned into a big tree on his way home from work.

Tommy and his sister were absent from school as they were suffering from conjunctivitis. I kept them off for a couple of days to keep an eye on them.

A boy had been sent home with a note from the school nurse informing his parents that he had nits in his hair and that they should follow the instructions on the bottle of shampoo. Next day came a short reply: 'It is the school's job to put something into his head, not to tell others how to take things out!'

I don't care what you right on his report card I no he is not stubid.

Sorry my son was off school last week when you were doing the eye cue test.

William's skin trouble is not termites (dermatitis) as we first thought.

Please excuse David for being off last week. He was in bed with diarrea for three days and it took him another three days to get over it.

Peter was absent from school yesterday as he had entered for the world record of 'how many times can one be sick over a twenty-four hour period.'

Your letter asking me to a meeting about the new school boards surprised me because I didn't think that blackboards should be the concern of the PTA.

Robert came home today and told us that a teacher had said that he was illiterate. I have to tell you that this is not the case as we were married five years before we had him and have his birth certificate to prove it.

My husband and I feel that William should drop history as we both feel there is no future in it.

Peter stayed off because of bad pans in his head. We have always known that this was his week part.

I am sending this note because John will be late on account of his having to take his father's breakfast.

Bad punctuation, not a knighthood, gives us this letter:
Sir John stayed off because he cut his arm badly in a fight.

Patricia had to take the day off as we were flitting and had to take her with us.

When we took her to the doctor because of the palpitations we kept her at home. I have to tell you, however, that her heart is still beating.

When Lorna came home she had bad pains in her stomach so we kept her at home to see what would come out of it.

There is really no point in him doing French because if he follows in his father's footsteps he will never leave the farm.

Latin is a dead language anyway and as far as my son is concerned the longer it stays that way the better.

Lesley was absent yesterday because she had an upset tammy.

Sorry Eric was absent this morning as he was extremely sick after breakfast. P.S. I am not a very good cook yet.

I must inform you that Julie McFarlane lost her peace, she says it was stollen. I am telling you because I do not want it to become a habbit.

Sometimes the pupils' excuses are equally amusing:

Please sir my mother was making jam and I had to go to the cemetery for jars.

I was off because my mother went to hospital to get me a wee brother. I'm back because it's a sister I've got and my father's got my auntie to live with us just now. He's going to try and get me a wee brother.

I went home to find out what time it was, that's why I was late, sir.

Please sir it wasn't me, Tommy did it with me.

Minor Mistakes

A couple of little girls were boasting about how much they were allowed to do around the house to 'help' their mum. One said that she laid the table every night for dinner and helped peel potatoes. 'That's nothing,' piped up the other, 'I'm allowed to make my own toast AND I'm allowed to scrape it myself.'

Two older pupils came into the school during the interval half carrying an infant, who was rubbing his leg as if in great pain. 'It was a big black labrador, Miss,' said the little lad. 'Did it bite you ?' asked the concerned teacher. 'No, Miss, it just tasted me,' whimpered the infant.

Talking about what they might do when they grew up, one little lad thought that being a fireman or an engine driver would be a bit boring. 'I want to be a teacher,' he shouted out, 'so that I can boss people about.'

When a four-year-old, who was the youngest of four boys, returned home from his first day at school, his mother asked him, 'Well, did you have a nice time today?' 'Yes, I did,' he replied. 'And did you make some friends?' 'Yes,' he said. 'And what were they called?' After thinking for a minute, the little fellow replied, 'I think they were called girls.'

The infant mistress decided to move round the groups of newly enrolled pupils just as the last of the mothers were leaving the classroom. Seeing one little girl looking a bit sad, she sat down in an empty chair beside her. Before the teacher could offer any words of encouragement, the lass piped up, 'Has your mummy just gone too?'

Twins had just arrived in the class and the teacher said, 'Well, boys, how am I going to tell you apart?' 'That's easy,' chirped up one of them, 'He's got a hamster, and I haven't!'

After what the teacher considered to be a very interesting lesson, she was more than a little dismayed when none of the children wished to comment or ask any questions. 'Have you no questions at all you want to ask?' she said. 'Please Miss, can we ask any question?' 'Certainly Susan, anything.' There was a pause and a giggle and then, 'Please Miss, do you know that you've got a big black hair on your chin?'

The little girl was being given a writing lesson, the teacher holding her hand and guiding it across the page. 'Now you try it, Jenny,' she said, letting go of her hand. 'But the pencil won't go, Miss,' she replied with a puzzled look on her face.

Mothers are often more upset than their offspring when they have to leave them at school on the first day. Clearly this was the case with one parent, when a little girl played with her friends while her mother hovered around anxiously in the background. After a while, the girl said, 'Don't worry, Mum, you can go home now, I'll come and see you at lunchtime.'

The headmaster called briefly to speak to the infant teacher with her new class. As he was leaving, one little fellow tugged at the teacher and asked, 'Please, Miss, what's He for?'

The headteacher was visiting the new intake for the first time and was walking round the room to see what they were doing. He approached a little boy in the Wendy House but when he spoke to him the wee lad turned and walked away with, 'My mum says that I've not to talk to strange men.'

The infant teacher was taking her new class round the school to show them where everything was. When they came to the dining room, one little lad piped up, 'Teacher, is this where we get our bar lunch?'

A little boy was given a row at the breakfast table by his mother. He ran upstairs, crying and shouting that he wasn't going to school and hid under the bed. When his dad appeared at the table he asked what the row was about and then went upstairs to have a word with his son. To humour the lad a little he crawled under the bed beside him. Before he could say anything, the boy, drying his tears, chipped in with, 'Has she given YOU a row too dad?'

The teacher was giving one little lad a row for getting so wet at play time. 'I told you to stay away from the puddles,' she said, taking him by the scruff of the neck.
'But, Miss, it was the puddle that jumped up on me from somebody else, as I walked past.'

When the five-year-old was asked why he was getting a holiday from school he replied casually, 'The teachers are all away being serviced.'

Having been told that a noun was a person, place or thing, a pupil gave as an example 'an organist'. Thinking it to be an unusual reply, the teacher asked why he had chosen that word. 'Because that's a person that plays a thing, isn't it?'

It was the five-year-old's first day at school and when he was introduced to the infant teacher she showed him to his seat in the classroom. He never said a word throughout the whole morning session but the patient teacher did not force him to join in with the others but left him to his own devices amongst the toys, assuming he would come round. He looked around the toys, equipment and pictures while the teacher talked to groups of children. Only occasionally, when she gently scolded a child, did the little fellow raise his head, look at her and frown. Towards the end of the day, when she hoped he would have settled down, she was pleased to see him approaching her desk to say something. He shocked the prim infant teacher with, 'This is a hell of a place this, I'm going home, and I'll not be back.'

The infant teacher had the new entrants line up to go on their first visit to the gym. Setting off along the corridor, she was aware that a little boy had started to whistle merrily. When she asked him to stop, he asked 'Why?'
'Well Paul,' she said, just think if I had to allow everyone to whistle along the corridor, what a noise there would be.' Whereupon he retorted, 'Well miss, don't let the rest of them whistle while I'm whistling.'

On her second day at school a little girl was standing quietly at the front of the school long after all the pupils had gone home. Thinking she was looking for her mother the janitor spoke to her. He was amused when she replied, 'No, I always go home myself, but I'm just looking to see where my teacher goes at night.'

My big brother has gone off to a bearding school.

'My Grandpa has bald hair.'

The class teacher was very interested to notice that the seven-year-old had cut out the multiplication tables from an old jotter and pasted them on to her own. However, when she enquired as to why she had only taken up to the five times table, the little girl boldly replied, 'Well, miss, I'll do these before I leave this school and I'll do the rest when I go to University.'

The teacher had repeatedly checked the girl in her class of five-year-olds for chattering while she was talking to the group. When she started whispering and giggling again she made her stand up and tell the whole class what she was whispering about. Reddening a little the lass, amidst giggles, said, 'I was only telling Susan that I thought you were awful fat.'

A small boy sent to the headmaster for swearing refused to tell the man what he had said and why. Anxious to find out the gravity of the offence, he insisted that the boy tell him and the little lad exclaimed, 'But, sir, I can't say it in front of you,' then added quietly, seeing that the headmaster was still angry, 'but if you tell me a few swear words yourself, I'll tell you when you come to it.'

A pupil, observed fidgeting during a lesson, was taken to task by the teacher, who enquired what he was playing with. The boy went red but made no reply. 'Please miss it's a pin he's got,' a little girl piped up and the offending article was taken away by the teacher from the boy's hand. Later on, when the teacher asked the boy to stand up and read, he reddened again and looked a little frightened. He was normally keen to read out, so she asked him what the matter was. 'Well miss, that pin you took keeps my trousers up.'

A small boy was asked to paint a radiator for a class frieze. (The other children were painting other classroom objects.) The teacher found his paper untouched, but the class radiator was a lovely green colour!

The harassed infant mistress, flinging open the door of the infants' toilet, announced, 'Now I'm coming to smack the next bottom that makes a noise in here!'

A little girl was asked why her sister didn't come home with her on the school bus. 'She'll be a long time and won't be home for ages yet,' was the reply. 'Why not?' asked her mother. 'Well, she has been picked as extra prostitute for the netball team because there's one short,' was the answer.

A little girl was asked by her teacher where the dot was that should have gone over the 'i' in her composition. The girl said, 'Oh that's still in the pencil.'

'I hope you will all have a good holiday now boys and girls and come back with some sense in your heads,' the teacher said as the class stood ready to go. 'Same to you, miss,' they replied in unison.

An elderly man passing a school playground took a boy to task for being cheeky to him and said, 'You deserve a good thrashing. I wish I was your father.' 'You can be if you like,' came the reply, 'My mother's a widow.'

The little girl ran home as fast as she could after her first day at school. 'I'm the prettiest girl in the class Mummy.' 'Who told you that?' the mother asked, laughing. 'Well,' she replied, 'I was there; I saw the others.'

When Mummy is angry, she puts on a teacher's voice. She sort of talks like a lady.

‘Well, what did you learn at school today?’ the young mother asked her son after his first day at school. ‘Nuffing,’ came back the reply, ‘I’ve got to go back tomorrow.’

There were hisses from the class when one of their mates presented the teacher with a lovely bunch of flowers. ‘How dare you make fun of John for being so kind,’ scolded the teacher. ‘You must have a lovely garden, John.’ ‘No miss,’ came the quick reply, ‘we haven’t got a garden, but I do a milk round in the morning.’

The pupil was clearly ashamed to admit that his father was an undertaker when asked about his parent’s profession. He neatly evaded the awkward question with, ‘Please Sir, he follows the medical profession.’

My daddy has bought a waist disposal unit for my mum.

‘Daniel, do you need the toilet?’ ‘No miss, I’m only warming my feet.’

‘What do tigers eat?’ ‘Frosties.’

I didn’t kick Peter first, I missed!

‘What is the desert full of, Tom?’ ‘Camels?’

‘Is there a special time when you eat turkey?’ ‘Yes miss, when it’s dead.’

A cemetery is where dead people live.

A little lad, always anxious to pass on a tale about another pupil, approached the teacher’s desk after the interval with, ‘Charlie never done the toilet.’ The teacher, more anxious about the grammar than the apparent misdemeanor replied, ‘Now Tommy, is it “did”, “done” or “went”?’ ‘Oh yes Miss, he went but he never done it.’

Billy, age five, said that he was going to his Granny’s for his holidays. The teacher was a little concerned because the school break had not begun. How long will you be off, Billy?’ After some deliberation he replied, ‘I’m not sure Miss, but I’ll tell you when I get back.’

‘Did I see you writing on the wall, Peter?’ ‘No Sir, I was drawing.’

From as infant 'News Book'; the saga starts two weeks before the birthday.

14 days to go: It is my birthday soon. I hope to get a horse.

12 days to go: Mummy says she likes horses too.

8 days to go: I can't wait to get a horse for my birthday.

3 days to go: Daddy says horses cost a lot of money.

2 days to go: I will call it Prince if it is a boy.

Birthday: I got a hamster for my birthday. It is called Goldy.

The day after: Mummy is scared of Goldie. Daddy helps me to hold it. I think Mummy would have liked a horse better.

The Head Teacher was showing two new infants around his school, chatting to them about the school rules and stressing how important it was for them to always do what the teachers told them. Suddenly he saw a pupil racing at full tilt along the corridor and shouted at the top of his voice, 'NEIL!!!' Instantly, the two youngsters at his side knelt down! He has been frightened of his power ever since.

John was very envious of the fact that his big brother, much older than he, was allowed out late at night to go to the cinema. In his 'News Book' he wrote: 'Colin gets to go to the pictures and is allowed up till he gets back.'

On his first day at school one little lad asked to go to the toilet. The infant teacher showed him where it was and returned to her room nearby. Presently the classroom door was pushed open by the same boy with his trousers round his ankles: 'Whose job is it about here to wipe bottoms?'

When the teacher was listening to one of her pupils reading at her desk, the child said, 'Please Miss, you smell like my baby brother!' She was taken aback, then she realised that she too used baby powder. Next day it was back to a more delicate fragrance after her shower!

Three answers from infants who were asked what we call a man who cuts down trees.
1. Peter's Dad.
2. A hatchet man.
3. A woodpecker.

'Tell me,' said the Headmaster to the class of first infants, 'Can anyone in this room read yet?' There was a pause. 'Yes, the teacher, Sir.'

The little girl seemed delighted to announce that she knew for certain that her mother's age was either 34 or 36. 'How do you know, Elizabeth?' the teacher enquired. She giggled for a bit and then revealed that she had seen an item of her mother's underwear and had read her age on the label. After all, didn't all her own clothes have 'Age 5-7' on the back!

The teacher wasn't sure how to react when a seven-year-old in her class declared 'I wish I was Gay.' Before she could open her mouth to speak, he continued, ' . . . she's got a horse and lives on a farm.'

'Now Susan, what does this letter say?' 'Please Miss, I've never heard it say anything.'

Teacher to a farmer's son: 'What would your father do if he had a field that was flooded? (Hopefully awaiting 'drain it'.) 'Keep out of it, Miss.'

Why do we keep zoo animals in cages? To keep the people out, Miss.

The infant teacher had already dismissed her pupils after their first day at school and had seen them safely off the premises. She returned to her classroom to find one little girl sobbing in her seat. 'Whatever is the matter, Jenny?' she enquired, putting her arm around her. 'Mummy says I've to stay here until I'm sixteen.' was the worried reply.

When I grow up I'm going to marry a shriek with lots of money.

Mummy, I got a reading book today but it's not nearly as good as the one you read to me at night. This one keeps using the same words.

'It's 25th January.Whose birthday is it today?' asked the teacher who normally sang 'Happy Birthday' for any of the pupils whose birthday fell on a school day, but had hoped that someone would remember Scotland's national bard. There was a long pause. 'Haven't you heard of Robert Burns?' 'He's not in this class, Miss,' a wee lad in the front quickly exclaimed.

The innocence of childhood can also have an effect on discipline, as the following story illustrates: The Headmaster was watching a group of infants, newly enrolled that morning, playing happily together. From the window he saw one of them suddenly begin to punch and kick another child. Anxious, not only to stop the fight but to assert his authority with a new pupil, he quickly went outside and marched the child towards his study. Swinging the door open ahead of the little boy he had no time to say anything before, in all innocence the lad said, looking up coyly, 'This is a nice house, who lives here?'

The teacher was discussing 'People who help us.' and the subject at that moment was the doctor.
'What does the doctor do for you?'
'Gives you pills when you are sick, Miss.'
One little lad interjected, 'When I'm sick my Mummy runs for a bowl!'

The name of Roberson Cruso's friend was Good Friday.

Colin's new duffle coat had been put on the cloakroom floor, not on the pegs as he had been clearly instructed, so the teacher was rather annoyed when she was told about it. 'And you just walked over it . . .' 'No, Miss, I jumped over it,' was the indignant reply.

The teacher was talking about famous people, pop stars, T.V. personalities etc. One little girl did not seem to be interested and appeared to be dreaming, so, as every good teacher is trained to do, she asked her a question to involve her. 'What would you like to do if you were a star, Susan?' Her quick and half-dazed reply was 'Twinkle, Miss!'

It was Christmas lunch at the little village school and the teacher gave a lecture on eating all the lovely food that had been prepared for them, particularly when boys and girls in many parts of the world were going hungry. The teacher ended with ' . . . and it's chicken today!' As quick as a flash the gamekeeper's son piped up, 'Thank goodness, I'm fed up with pheasant.'

A teacher, supervising the dining hall noticed that a plate had been pushed into the centre of the table with the vegetables untouched. Six five-year-olds were sitting at the table and she asked them whose plate it was in an attempt to get the child to at least eat some. But she tried in vain as they all denied that it was their plate. However, an older girl, the sister of one of the children came over to ask what was wrong. One of the youngsters replied in a loud voice, 'I left my vegetables and the teacher wants to know who did it.'

The class was suddenly interrupted by a gigantic sneeze from a little girl at the back of the room. 'Susan, what do you say?' asked the teacher. 'Bless me, Miss,' was the quick reply.

I am Jimmy. I love my Mother. I love my Father. I love my Sister. I love my Dog. I love my Budgie. But not all of them love me.

Teacher: 'Now boys and girls, you will have to be on your toes for this one.' At this, the children stood up.

I like bacon, but not when it's rusty.

The little boy excitedly announced to his teacher that his mummy had brought a baby boy back from the hospital. 'And what is his name?' asked the teacher. 'I think it's Spot,' he replied. 'That's an interesting name,' said the teacher, diplomatically. Later that day when Dad called at the school he said to the teacher, 'I suppose John has told you the news?' 'We're calling him Mark.'

The infant class were singing the children's song: I've got a little light, I'm going to let it shine, Let it shine, Let it shine, Let it shine. 'The battery will run out,' said one concerned little boy.

Every infant teacher used to reversals of letters when teaching will appreciate this one:
Teacher: 'What should you do when you discover fire?
Child: 'Dial P.P.P.'

A primary class visited the local library. The teacher anxious to imbue an interest in reading told the class to pick any book.
Child clutching very heavy tome: 'Please Miss, who is this guy Harold Pinter?'
Teacher (slightly surprised): 'He is a very, very good writer.'
Child (thinks for a moment and then): 'Does that mean he can do his W's?'

We don't have sheets or blankets on our beds now. Mummy bought two lovely soft bidets.

'Doreen, has your mother got a washing machine?'
'She's got two, Miss. One that wets the clothes and one that drys them.'

Writing Wrongs

A solicitor is someone who breaks up your marriage and charges you for it.

Every American President shows his respect for his country. He stands up, swears, and salutes the stars and strips.

Another name for a 'public conveyance' is a toilet.

In a lesson on the comparison of adjectives, the teacher set the class some examples to work out, among them being 'ill'. One rather pessimistic pupil wrote, 'ill, worse, dead.'

'Please Miss, how do you spell "fought"?'
'Do you mean as in "two boys fought in the playground," Susan?'
'No, Miss, I mean the fought you fink in your head.'

A down bed is a bed on the floor.

Terra Cota is stuff squeezed out of little insects and used to turn puddings red.

My father is a civil serpent.

What is dusk? Little bits of fluff that fly about in the air.

The old man kept lots of ancient things in his house. He was specially interested in old bras. Round the fireplace he had nailed lots of old bras of different shapes and sizes taken from his farm horses.

A rhetorical question is a question you know there is no answer to like, 'What has the government been doing since it came into power?'

Pit ponies sadly sometimes end up in a knickers yard.

Irrigation is when the farmer wets the field himself.

Another name for a bird watcher is a naturist.

The lady was very poor. When her husband died she asked the welfare to arrange a state funeral for him.

When the writer spoke of a 'hire car' he probably wanted one that gave him a better view.

Q. Define the first person.
A. Adam.

All the teachers in our school are certified.

'Inflation in the country is caused by . . .?' 'A lot of hot air, Sir.'

A good friend says nasty things to your face, not behind your back.

'Lingerie' means hanging about.

There is no doubt that people on television are uncovered in the most unexpected places so it is really worth the cost of the licence fee.

The Victoria Cross is a woman given to soldiers if they are good.

I stood on the cliff, the sea was rough and the wind roared and not a sole was to be seen.

A sure-footed animal is one which does not miss when it kicks you.

Chivalry is when you feel cold.

It was a nice house, but the drains were unfit for human habitation.

The son came shinning in at the window.

Nets are holes surrounded by pieces of string.

He had no difficulty getting out as he knew the building like the back of his head.

Cereals are stories that go on and on.

An obituary is a home for lady dogs.

Gender tells you when a man is masculine, feminine or neuter.

The tyres were solid in those days and really hurt you when you went out and got cobbled.

Speedway riders must have nerves of steel, otherwise they would get killed, which is my ambition in life.

An anenome is a person who fights against you.

A tantrum is a kind of two seater bicycle.

A spectre is a man who goes to football matches.

If you didn't go to school you wouldn't learn good.

A martyr is someone who suffers for his or her briefs.

The people who lived in the country came into the town for special services such as hairdressing, banking and soliciting.

After being in the Brownies for some time you are publicly unrolled.

The expression used is 'Don't upset the apple tart'.

Necessity is the mother of convention.

Today many people are in jail for committing suicide while under the influence of drink.

Seafaring men in the habit of drinking are liable to collide with other vessels.

What is a mediator? A man who says, 'Punch me instead.'

If a man takes alcohol, his wife and children suffer, and vice versa.

A surname is the name of a person you say 'Sir' to.

Everyone needs a holiday from one year's end to another.

A conjunction is a place where two railway lines meet.

Write a sentence showing clearly the meaning of 'posterity'. The cat leaped about and then sat on its posterity.

A fort is a place to put men in, a fortress is a place to put women in.

Many new faces toed the line at the school marathon.

In the eighteenth century travelling was very romantic, most of the high roads were only bridal paths.

Sailors do not like the sea when it is rough because it is very dangerous and many lives are lost and few of them found again.

A talisman is a man who calls every week for the furniture money.

A parsimonious boy is a boy who wants to be a parson.

A hostage is a big bird that buries its head in the sand.

Our food was eaten and our water was drunken.

It was simply a pigment of his imagination.

A skeleton is a man with his inside out and his outside off.

Man is the only animal who can strike a light.

The different kinds of senses are commonsense and nonsense.

A blood vessel is a man's lifeboat.

The home of the swallow is the stomach.

A fissure is a man who catches fish.

You cannot tell the gender of 'egg' until it is hatched.

The Press today is the mouth-organ of the people.

I searched for the missing book in every room and in each case the search was fatal.

A phlegmatic person is one who has chronic bronchitis.

Polonius was a mythical sausage.

He was standing on the water's edge, striped to the waist.

The woman always had plenty of money and it was clear that she was living off her immoral earings.

Write a sentence using the word straightforward.
My nose goes straight forward on my face.

He had a wide sombrero neatly erected on his head.

Her beautiful hare fell on to her bear shoulders.

It was my turn to be severed in the meat queue.

A backbiter is another name for a flea.

Sailors in the navy can be noticed because they wear feeders on the back of their necks.

One form of execution in the United States is the electric cushion.

I was so excited that I ran home and toweled my father.

We climbed into the crib to see where many famous people were buried.

We were amazed to see Ivy climbing up the outside of the house and in the window.

We were so tired that we just had a big cup of hot chocolate and fell in.

She lived in a large house on the superbs of the town.

No talking is aloud!

He was hot and thirsty so he sat down by a wayside inn and had a tanker of beer.

When an old man thinks of his young days he will think it ignorance to think silly things he knows better of now.

In the distance we noticed a large field of fur trees.

The police took very large steps to trap the road hog.

He sacrificed his life many times for his country.

'Rat tat tat,' went the front door bell.

After the butler took in the old bags he introduced us to the rest of the family.

In olden days bores were hunted by dogs.

As we had plenty more time and it was a nice evening we decided to pull father out to see.

She now lies in peas in a beautiful churchyard.

Dog Rose and Horse Radish are plants called after animals. Can you think of any more? Collie Flower.

The Dodo is a bird that is nearly decent now.

The subject I lick best is speling.

There were over a hundred gusts at the party.

The Greek gods thought they were immoral so they had the time of their lives.

She laughed behind her breath.

There is a lot of punctuation in the story. It helps the rabbit to express its feelings to the horse.

Complete these proverbs:

Its an ill wind . . . that blows from the north; that does everybody good.

Two blacks . . . don't make a piece; sing as nice as swallows.

Every cloud . . . has rain in it; passes over in summer.

A stitch in time . . . stops you running; saves you mine.

A rolling stone . . . stops eventually; gathers the grass.

Record players used to be called grammar phones.

There are few pursuits that a man can rise higher in than mountaineering.

The teacher told us to sit on pears on the desks.

After a cordial farewell they climbed down the stars.

People who eat vegetables are called vergens.

Without cows we would have to go around in bear feet.

The baby lamps sat all over the field at night.

A post graduate is another name for a dead teacher.

The antique dealer gave us a running commentary on the table.

Because some of the old people in the home cannot climb the stairs they have built special wings for them.

I much prefer consecrated juice to artyficial.

He was well known as a truss worthy man.

When you sneeze you should use atishoo paper.

My father has taken out a life membership of the national truss.

He was a tall seafearing man who loved boats.

Dew is a sort of spittle on the grass in the morning.

On Saturday we went to a jungle sale in the church hall.

A gargoyle is a liquid used for a throatwash.

It was a big old house with ivory growing up the outside of the walls.

She was swept away by a huge currant.

I had to go and get a massage for my mother.

The flames were coming up from the celery below. They had already burned away the ground floor.

Every man on the sinking ship was shaved including the ships cat.

There is nothing better than real daisy ice cream.

I play the villain in the pantomime, but I don't mind the hisses and the booze.

Etiquette is the noise you make when you sneeze.

When the boy regained his conscience he landed up in hospital.

Q. Why does the author say that we should hold old people in respect?
A. Because they are the ones that generally have money.

There was not a sole on the boat until the kipper appeared from down below.

A beautiful paramour met his gaze as he reached the summit of the mountain.

We all went off in threes except for the two of us who went off in twos.

We went into a large hall in the school so that we could do Jim.

In winter it is often very cold and sadly many old people die and go to heaven. Animals generally end up in a warmer place.

He rushed over and gave the boy artificial perspiration.

'Now what would you find in air?' asked the science teacher.
'Please sir, Butlin's is in Ayr,' replied one pupil without hesitation, 'I was there for my holidays last year.'

'What part of the body is the trombone, Miss ?'
'That's not a part of the body, Anne.'
'It must be. The story says, "After the concert it was dark and the man tripped and fell on his way home, breaking his trombone." '

Sheep are sheared so they don't get hot in summer.

No pupil should leave school until he has mastered the basic three R's.

Mind Your Language

People who work for the government are called senile servants.

A navigator is the strap which a navvy wears under his knees to stop rats running up his leg.

When the airman came to the edge of the volcano he could see the creator smoking.

The appendix is part of a book for which no one has yet discovered a use.

Chequers is a public house belonging to the Prime Minister.

A welsher is a native of Wales.

To scotch something is to drown your sorrows in whisky.

A mosquito is the child of black and white parents.

Transparent is something you can see through. For example – a keyhole.

Acrimony is another name for marriage.

Polygamy is a shape with many sides to it.

A pagoda is a chair on wheels used for carrying people about.

To be 'called to the Bar' is to be treated to a drink.

'Unaware' means your vest and pants.

The Last Post is always sounded by a lone burglar.

'The cat is a quadruped, the legs as usual being at the four corners. Do not tease cats, because firstly, it is wrong to do so and secondly, because of his clawses which is longer than people think. Cats have nine lives, but it is seldom required in this country because of Christianity.'
'Now children,' said the teacher, 'I want you to write me a story. Something different. Something you haven't thought of before. Write what is inside

you at this very moment.' One of the stories ran: 'Inside of me there is my heart, my liver, lots of other parts and of course the mince and stewed prunes I had for dinner.'

'Where would you put the colon?' 'On the fire, sir.'

A kite is a light wooden frame covered with paper and is sent into the air by boys with tails on them.

Everyone staying in the house on the day of the census must be filled in or else.

The man found hanging outside the bank was acting in a peculiar way.

My mum uses polythene for my dad's food.

People go self cantering at Butlin's Holiday Camp.

We have got a new home copulator.

The sponsored walk was organised by the school to help cripple children.

A man with a wife and two children got about five times as much as a man not married with no children so men were desperately trying to get married and to get lots of children.

In 19th century Britain because of the squalor, people found they were going back instead of forward.

The company turned into a liquid to pay off its debts.

When the X-ray van came we had to take off some of our clothes in a cuticle.

They are putting up a new building in town for the farewell officers.

I like Mrs McKinnon, she gives us pea tea.

A deacon is something you put on a hill and set fire to it.

‘Give a sentence including “human race”.’ ‘My dad ran in the human race.’

I felt sacred as I walked to the dentist’s.

A cloister is when things are bundled up together.

Luxury means when you like it and cuddle down to it.

Massacre is black stuff people put on their eyes.

Amphibious – a Greek God.

Pluto took Persephone on the Underground.

Why are there inverted commas around ‘patient’? So that the blood will flow easily into the bottle placed tactfully under the bed.

A white collar worker is a lavadry cleaner.

A young horse is called a clot.

From a letter of application: ‘Perhaps you would like to see me in your convenience?’

Aquamarine – a soldier specialising in underwater swimming.

A deaf mute is a deaf dog.

Inspired means they had it coming to them.

Q. Give the masculine equivalent of the following: Filly.
A. Empty.

I must draw a one-inch virgin on the left-hand side of the page.

Plumb: A thing that cleans drains out; fattish.

The king wore a scarlet robe trimmed with vermin.

The men of the little fishing village used their wives to bait their lines. Although it was sore they did not mind. Sometimes however they mended their nuts.

Immobile: mobile means to make smaller e.g. a mobile library, so immobile means to make larger.

Neap: A drink without water in it; A pile of something; Tidy; Large.

Palpable: squashable; to mash.

Silhouette: to turn round on the spot.

Hamlet: a little eggs beaten up with some bacon.

A paltry attempt: a place where you try to keep hens.

They had 325 guests and relations for dinner at the reception.

Illustrate the difference between two, to and too. There are two o's in too but only one in two and to.

Another type of wood is hogmanay.

A rudder is used for milking cows.

Monogamy is a kind of furniture.

'What does "saddest" mean?' 'Wood after it has been sad.'

Proverbs: One swallow doesn't make a dram. Never look a gift horse up the nose. Fine feathers make fine cushions.

During a spelling lesson the teacher wrote the words 'widow' and 'window' on the board. 'Now children,' she said, 'I want you to notice the difference between "widow" and "window". What is it?' 'Please, miss,' was the answer, 'we can see through a window, but we can't see through a widow.'

In the older days they danced round the maypole in May, especially on Mayday. They do not do it now because they call it Labour.

Mayday used to be celebrated by Labour, now it is used by airmen and sailors when they want help.

In spring our local farmer spreads new seeds to feed the crows.

The bride wore orange blossom as a symbol of innocence, purity and future abundance.

When my feet are wet I take them off and dry them at the fire.

A cuckoo is a bird which lays other birds' eggs in its own nest.

When coal runs out we will have to use our brains for fuel.

The plural of ox is oxo. The plural of forget-me-not is forget-us-not.

A relative pronoun is a family pronoun such as 'mother', 'brother' and 'aunt'.

A rhinoceros is so called because rind means skin and nocerous nose.

Spelling errors are often unconsciously humorous:

My Daddy is a shosho worker (social worker).

A ruminating animal is one which chews its cubs.

Rapids are animals with long ears and nearly no tails.

A mandoline was a high official in China.

At the end of the long race the horse dropped with fatigue and the poor rider was pitched into maternity.

Know Your Authors

Shakespeare was a very polite man. He often said 'Go to . . .' but never finished the sentence.

Most of Shakespeare's plays are terrible tragedies.

Shakespeare made a mistake in mentioning Galen, who did not live till a hundred years after his time.

In Shakespeare's play Omlet, we read that . . .

One of Shakespeare's plays was called *Charlie's Aunt*.

Shakespeare's father could not afford to give him a good education so he sent him to Oxford.

Hamlet was the town where the rats invaded.

Shakespeare probably wrote Henry IV in two parts to leave room for the commercials.

Milton was made Poet Orient.

Chaucer lived in London. He translated the Bible, and was put in jail. After doing nothing for some time, he came to the conclusion that he might as well write another book, and then wrote *Pilgrim's Progress*.

In 1620 the Pilgrim Fathers crossed the ocean. This was called the Pilgrim's Progress.

Pope wrote chiefly in cutlets.

Virgil was in love with a girl called Enid and wrote a lot of books about her.

James Joyce is famous for his book *All Sizes*.

Plato was the God of the Underground.

The poem of the Forsaken Merman made me very angry, to think a woman could leave a poor helpless man to get his own meals.

'The lark that soars on dewy wing' means that the lark was going so high and flapping its wings so hard that it broke into perspiration.

Do you think Shylock was necessarily a bad character? No, because after all, he had his living to make.

George Bernard Shaw was a famous actor and comedian.

Hans Christine Anderson was a very famous Danish writer.

If it says 'anon' at the end of a poem it generally means that the author did not know who wrote it.

A philosopher is a man who makes the best of a bad job. Socrates is called a philosopher because he didn't worry much when he was poisoned.

Sir Walter Scott was known as the Blizzard of the North. He failed in his attempt to reach the North Pole.

One of his plays was 'A Sidecar Named Desire'.

Tennyson wrote a book called *In Memorandum.*

Socrates died from an overdose of wedlock.

When Caesar died he said, 'Ate two Brutes'.

If it had not been for the love of liquor, Burns might have been with us yet.

After twice committing suicide, Cowper lived till 1800 when he died a natural death.

Charles Lamb is my favourite author. He had touches of insanity.

What do you know about Keats? I don't even know what a Keat is.

The well known poem begins: 'Seasons of mists and melon fruitfulness . . .'

Triangles and Test Tubes

Geometry teaches us to bisect angels.

A theorum – derived from theos a god and res a thing – is a problem demanding divine intelligence.

Algebraic symbols are used when you don't know what you are talking about.

Geometry teaches us to prove what we already know to be true.

Things which are halves of themselves are equal to each other.

Parallel lines, even if produced to eternity, cannot expect to meet unless you bend them.

If two triangles have two sides of the one equal to three angles of the other, each to each, to which the opposite sides are also equal, the triangles shall be equal in all respects.

The hypoteneuse is the line which when someone saw when he was having a bath he shouted, 'I've found it!' and ran out naked to tell everyone.

A circle is a round straight line with a hole in the middle.

Q: The electrolyte used in the manufacture of aluminium has a very high melting point. How is this lowered?
A: Using a crane.

The blood consists of red and white corkscrews.

If you did not eat for sixty days you would die within a month.

An average is something that hens lay on.

The best way to keep milk from going sour is to keep it in the cow.

A fatal disease is the worst type you can have.

Sir Isaac Newton invented gravity when an apple fell on his head.

Water is composed of two gins; oxygin and hydrogin.

X rays are produced when the sun's rays cross each other.

Because hot air rises it is warmer at the top of a mountain.

The weather at the North Pole is so bad that the towns there are not inhabited.

The effect of lead in water is that it sinks in it.

Teacher to pupils: 'This is an axle in my hand. At the end of this axle is a crank. Pupil: 'Which end, sir?'

To remove air from a flask, pour the water out and put the cork in quick.

A magnetic force is a straight line, generally a curved one, which would tend to point to where the North Pole comes.

Mechanically a long pump handle is better because you can get someone to help you.

Ammonium chloride is also called silly maniac.

Air is made up of oxygen and sanatogen.

CO_2 is used for keeping people from dyeing and distinguishing fires.

A curve is the longest way between two points.

To fill an apparatus with acidulated water, turn on the taps and acidulate.

What does nitric acid do? It burns yellow holes in your clothes.

How do nuclear scientists avoid the effects of radiation? They sit well back from the fire.

Oxygen has eight sides.

A thermometer is for measuring how much water there is in milk, a hydrometer for measuring how much milk there is in water.

To germinate is to become a naturalised German.

A circle is a round line with no kinks in it, joined up so as not to show where it began.

An alkali is a chemical substance without water in it, like whisky.

What are nitrates? They are cheaper than dayrates.

The difference between 'mass' and 'weight' is that when you buy a sack of potatoes that is 'mass'. 'Weight' is when you carry it home.

The animal which has the greatest attachment to man is woman.

It is wise to get intoxicated before you go abroad to keep away strange diseases.

A vacuum is just another name for a Hoover.

Trees that stay green all year round are called artificial.

After an experiment during a science lesson, the teacher asked the class to write in their jotters what they had discovered. One child wrote, 'We discovered it was all very difficult.'

Newton discovered that when an apple becomes over ripe it falls to the ground.

In a country school the teacher always tried to relate the work to the general knowledge of the children. The gamekeeper's son was having difficulty with simple multiplication. 'If a salmon weighed five kilos and it was sold at 10p a kilo, what would it be worth?' asked the teacher. 'It wouldn't be worth buying at that price!' came the informed reply, 'Unless it had been poached.'

Charles weighs 6 stone 12 inches.

'Come out all the mental people,' said the teacher to the arithmetic class.

Horse-power is the distance one horse can carry a pound of water in an hour.

A centimetre is an insect with a hundred legs.

'How would you hatch eggs without the aid of a hen?'
'Use a duck.'

Germs are small insecks that swim inside you when they can get in. Some are called measles, but you can't see them.

Anaemia is not having enough blood, but you have enough to bleed as much as anyone else if you cut your finger.

Every Spring our house is invaded by house martians.

Our teeth will go bad if you let the air get on to them.

Why is this year called a Leap Year? Because it is the one year when a woman can 'leap' at a man.

'Which is more, half an orange or eight sixteenths?' was the trick question given to the class.
'Half,' answered one smart fellow. 'You would lose more juice cutting it into sixteen bits.'

Pure water must contain hydrogen because oxygen would just float away if it was not for the hydrogen.

The spinal chord keeps the back from doubling over and if the brain is injured it does the work of the brain.

It is ill eagle to steal birds' eggs from a nest.

My uncle in Caithness is a New Clear Santas.

You use a sandglass to boil eggs in.

When you look at a camel the first thing that strikes you is the huge hump. When you look closely the next thing that strikes you is the big hoofs.

One seven-year-old was heard to remark just before a science lesson, 'Oh great, its science. I wonder if we'll have an experience?'

'If I cut a piece of meat into sixteenths and then cut these pieces in three parts, what would I have?' asked the teacher. 'Mince, sir.'

If we are not careful, decimals can burst our ear drums.

A person who doesn't eat any fish, meat, eggs or plants and vegetables is called a vegan.

The Mail Order Protection Scheme means that you cannot try on underwear from a catalogue before you buy it.

In the stomach the food is turned round and round and gets mixed up with ghastly juices.

When they erupt, lots of lager flows out of volcanoes.

A lion is really just a tiger with black and white dots.

When buying a pair of cutting out shears it is important to consider what they sound like.

For school dinners we get low fat jelly for pudding.

The camel is known as 'the sheep of the desert'.

The teacher filled the brunette from the science lab. with alcohol.

Hardly Historical

The teacher warned the class not to spend a lot of time writing about Alfred burning the cakes in the swineherd's house but to tell of his work for the people and welfare of his country. When the exam came along one girl wrote: 'Alfred, among other things which he did, paid a visit to the cottage of a swineherd's wife but the less that is said about this the better.'

Julius Caesar landed in Britain in 55 BC and went away in 410 AD.

In 1314 King Robert the Bruce won the Bannock of Battleburn.

Lord Nelson's last words at the Battle of Trafalgar as he waved his arms over the noise was, 'Peace be still'. When he had finished his last words he plunged his head into Captain Hardy's chest and all was over.

The Battle of Trafalgar Square was fought in London against the Spaniards.

During the Napoleonic Wars crowned heads were trembling in their shoes.

Mary Queen of Scots had no time to say her last words for her head came off too suddent.

History tells us that Oliver Cromwell was afraid of nothing except his wife.

During the Black Hole of Calcutta one hundred and forty-six men were confined all night in a cellar with one widow and in the morning only twenty-three staggered forth alive and they were romantic with thirst.

Clive imprisoned 146 men in the Black Hole of Calcutta and so laid the foundations for the British Empire.

Charles II told the people that they could now do as they pleased, get drunk or gamble. This was called the Restoration.

The Great Fire of London was caused by someone dropping a match into a tin of petrol in a garage.

Mary Queen of Scots married the Dolphin of France.

The Young Pretender was quite harmless, as was seen by the way he was hidden by the maid in Scotland.

The King of Spain was very angry when Columbus discovered America, but it wasn't Columbusses' fault. He didn't look for it, because he never new it was there. His boat just dunted into it.

Henry the Eighth was said to iron his trousers on his wife's back. ('Meanwhile, Henry was pressing his suit on Anne Boleyn.'!)

Who invented gunpowder? A lady who wanted guns to look nice.

The Highland Clearances was a big sale of sheep in the North of Scotland.

King William had a new forrest maid and he killed everyone who chased his dear.

Nelson had a column put up for him in Trafalgar Square. It is high so that everyone can see where he fell and remember him for his extinguished conduct for England.

James the First claimed the throne of England through his mother as he had no father to speak of.

Victoria was the longest queen that ever ruled in Britain. She was a good woman but I don't think she ever married. Her daughter was Queen Elizabeth.

At the Battle of Hastings William ordered his archers to shoot at the thickest part of the English so they shot upwards so that the arrows might fall on their heads.

During King John's reign England was placed under an interdict and the Pope stopped all births, marriages and deaths for a year.

The Magna Carta said that the King could not order taxis without the consent of parliament.

The Duke of Wellington had a splendid funeral. It took twelve men to carry the beer.

After Culloden Prince Charlie wandered the moors disguised as a pheasant.

The King's Pardon was what a woman got when she had triplets.

Columbus circumcised the world with a 40ft clipper. The church was against such things but the king of his country was all for it as it brought them fame and money.

Another name for the German Emperor was 'the Geyser'.

General Custer was the leader of the Roundheads.

During the American Wars of Independence, Lord Northcliffe wisely gave the Irish Volunteers Home Rule.

The Pope lives in the Vacuum.

The inflammability of the Pope was proclaimed in the Vatican Degrees.

The Glorious First of June was fought on June 1st.

Everybody was killed at the Battle of Edgehill but they all carried on fighting, and the cavalry advanced backwards.

The Romans came to Britain because there was no room at Rome.

Julius Caesar was a Greek ruler. He was Emperor. He must of been bonkers to burn down Rome, but when he was assassinated he could do nothing more.

Habeus Corpus was a man who died in battle.

Elizabethan men wore pointed goblets.

The Puritans did not like the Bishops to wear any clothing.

Q. What is a mummy? A. A body raped in fine linen, and reserved.

Q. When were the Middle Ages? A. 40 to 50.

Q. What was the Roman Forum? A. Something they sat on.

King Richard led a crusade to the Holy Land to fight the Saccharins.

Queen Elizabeth rode through Coventry with nothing on and Sir Walter Raleigh offered her his cloak. She later had him beheaded.

Mary Queen of Scots lost the Bottle of Langsyne near Glasgow in 1568.

The Bloody Statute was another name for Queen Mary. She was called this because she wouldn't talk.

The housewives of Paris sat and knitted while the guillemot did its deadly work.

Muskets were so heavy that musketeers would have a rest.

Some Puritans had three ears cut off.

You always knew if you had the plague because you died.

As the Spanish Fleet sailed into the English Channel, Drake said, 'The Armada can wait, my bowels can't.'

In Normandy they had Gateaux which were like castles and mansions put together.

Q. How did you know if you had the plague? A. There was a red cross on the door.

The Mayflower was the ship that was used to find the treasure in *Treasure Island*.

The tomb of Totem Carmen was opened in Egypt.

At the end of the year Mr Macmillan planed to reshape his cabinet.

The Japanese over-ran China and even occupied Formica.

Queen Victoria's husband was King Victoria.

Disraeli was a man of principle; he married a rich woman for her money.

Karl Marx was one of the famous Marx Brothers. He founded the International Working Mens Federation and had the misfortune to invent Communism.

Charles Colling bred Durham shorthorn cows with his brother Robert.

The Battle of Hastings was between William the Concera and Saladin. It was fort on Mount Carmel.

Napoleon complained that his soldiers marched on his belly.

The Luddites were given a capital punishment namely death.

Palestine was important because it layed on a camel root.

The Pilgrim Fathers did not find it easy to found a Colony as so many had been found already.

The Protestants disliked the smell of the incest in the Catholic Church.

The King sold foreign policies to make money.

Martin Luther was famous for his Diet of Worms. He said, 'Heaven help me I can take no other course.'

John Knox was born in Haddington, Scotland, little thinking he would become a great reformer.

Van Gogh committed suicide by cutting off his ear.

'Habeus corpus' means 'you may have the body'. This was during the Great Plague.

Wellington's nickname was Ironpants.

William the Conqueror spent a phew nights in Canterbury.

Henry II never wore clothes except when he was hawking.

The Spinning Jenny was worked by a cock which you knocked from one side of the machine to the other.

Victorian ladies had thrills around their bottoms.

The Puritans sometimes wore a white collar, but that was all.

Henry VIII quarrelled with the Pope because he marred his brother's wife.

In Tudor times women had square chests.

The return of Charles II to the throne was called the Resurrection.

Mungo Park led some kind of exhibition somewhere. He stopped a war or something.

Pompeii was destroyed in a night by an overflow of saliva.

Joan of Arc was burned to a steak for her good deeds.

In the political world today we are faced with the choice of Free Trade or Detection.

The Court of the Chancery is so called because there is not a chance that you will get your money back, when it has once been looked after by it.

George Washington was famous for wasting his father's plum tree and saying, 'Yes, I done it; I cannot tell a lie; thank God I have done my duty.'

The Root and Branch Bill ordered farmers to prune their trees every year.

The Peasants Revolt was caused by placing a poultice (poll tax) on the head of every person over sixteen.

For services rendered at Locarno, Sir Austen Chamberlain was knighted and his wife damed.

The Great Fire of London really did a great deal of good. It purged the city from the plague and burned down eighty-nine churches.

The Black Prince died of injuries received by his horse.

The Romans built Hadrian's Wall so they could jump over it and surprise the Scots.

The Navigation Act prohibited any goods from being exported except to the country where they were manufactured.

The crown was not passed on in his family because the king had no hair.

In 1918 there was a war and every year since we have had two minutes peace.

The South Sea Bubble was a scream for lending money to the government.

The low wages paid by the farmers led to the pheasants' revolt.

William the Conqueror was thrown from his horse and wounded in the Feudal System.

The Minister of War was a clergyman who preached to the soldiers in their barracks.

Simon de Montford formed what was known as the 'Mad Parliament'. It is something the same as we have at the present time.

William the Conqueror surrounded the Isle of Ely with his feet.

A crow at the mast-head of a French ship fired twice at Nelson and killed him.

Why does true English history begin with the reign of Henry VIII? Because up to this time it was all lies.

Guerilla warfare means up to their monkey tricks.

The budget is a list of grievances secretly presented to the Prime Minister to rectify the unemployed.

In the Middle Ages the monks went into other peoples houses and helped everybody, doing every man's work. About this time the population of England increased threefold.

He was given the crown of Scotland and a stone scone.

They called them 'The Dark Ages' because it was before electric light.

Joan of Arc was Noah's sister.

The Duke of Monmouth was found lying in a ditch, with some peas in his pocket which he had eaten.

At the Battle of Crecy the soldiers found a motor car (ford) which they used to cross the river.

Sir Winston Churchill was the first Prime Minister to use an iron curtain.

The Russian Revolution started when the people rose up against the tar.

Hitler said that he wanted to have a larger living room for his people.

Hitler and his wife were found dead in a coal bunker at the end of the war. They had just got married and he did not want to surrender.

The last shots of the First World War were fired in a railway carriage. We celebrate it with Armistice Day each year.

During the war silk was very scarce because it was all used for parshots.

The teacher told the class how, when General Wolfe stormed the Heights of Quebec, the soldiers rowed up the river in boats with muffled oars. One boy recorded this in his note book as 'the soldiers crept up the river with buffalos.'

Oliver Cromwell's nose was very large and a deep red colour but underneath it he was a very religious soul.

The Declaration of Indulgence in James's reign was when people were allowed to worship God in their own way. Seven bishops refused to do so and they were put on trial. They were found not guilty.

If the Premier dies, who officiates? An undertaker.

Where was the Magna Carta signed? At the bottom.

Napoleon lost his navel at the Battle of Waterloo.

With the Feudal System you had to lend each other your tractor.

Queen Elizabeth was pale and thin but she was a stout Protestant.

'Who said, "Kiss me Hardy"?' 'Laurel, Sir.'

The greatest thing about Oliver Cromwell was the wart on his nose.

The first Roman sent to Britain was very cross with the people for not being Christians.

Edward III would have been King of France if his mother had been a man.

Prisons in the Norman period were not like ours today. They were dull and dreary.

Robert the Bruce was a very brave leader who fought like a spider.

The Normans put moles around their castles to protect them from attack.

Where are the descendants of the ancient Britons to be found today? The British Museum.

Henry VIII had the Prayer Book put into English to spite the Pope, who wanted to marry Catherine of Arragon.

Prince Henry was drowned in the wash. The story goes that he never smiled again.

Henry had an abbess on his knee, which made walking difficult.

The Battle of Sluys was fought at sea. It was one of those battles in which the bowmen did better work than the cavalry.

Where were the Kings of Britain generally crowned? On their heads.

What do you know about Marconi? Marconi is used to make delicious puddings.

During the Great Fire of London, the worst flaming place of all was St Paul's Cathedral.

Lenin was the first revolting leader of Russia.

'Why was he called "God's silly vassal"?' 'I don't know, it seems a silly name to call anybody.'

Why did the industrial revolution start? Someone shot the Tsar.

If John Knox were alive today he would turn in his grave.

The Duke of Wellington got his name from the type of boots that he wore.

Stanley's first words were: 'Dr Limestone I presume?'

One of the greatest men to have lived in America was Martian Luther King.

Marie Antoinette said: 'Let them have their cake and eat it.'

The Battle of Haystrings was fought in 1066.

Speaking about pollution on the River Clyde, the teacher told the class that it was said that King Robert the Bruce once fished for salmon there. 'Why would he not be able to catch salmon today?' asked the teacher. 'Because he's dead, Miss!'

In the 1960's Beeching was forced to lift all the railway lines in order to make ends meet.

Perhaps the Normans were more mechanised than hitherto realised for one pupil wrote: They used a battery ram to attack castles and the Domesday Book was ordered by William I to work out the amount of taxis his subjects could afford.

Tollund Man was found when two men were digging for Pete.

Sir Walter Raleigh introduced tobacco and said, 'Today I have lit a fire in England that shall never be put out.'

Wellington was buried with full millinary honours.

The first wireless message came from a man that went through the air.

Cromwell died in constant fear of being murdered.

The monasteries were dissolved because monks liked gamboling.

In Germany the Nasty Party took over and ran all over Europe.

Mummies were Egyptians who buried themselves in bandages after they died so that they would live longer in the afterlife.

That type of farming suited middle aged people but they had to be prepared to work very hard.

Elizabeth Fry was a well known quacker.

Britain at that time had a very good navy and they were far better at fighting at sea than they were on land.

We do not know why Stonehenge was built, but it certainly was built for some porpoise.

The armour was so heavy in those days that knights had to be lifted on to their houses with a crane.

January is named after the Roman goddess Janice.

During the Medieval Period people were sent out on pilgrimages so that they might repeat their sins.

Samuel Pepys kept a dairy.

Where in the World

The whole world lies in a temperence zone except the United States.

Britain has a temporary climate.

The tropic of Cancer is a strange incurable disease.

In the Highlands distilling is the only industry carried to excess.

Crewe is the biggest conjunction in England.

London is by far the biggest polution centre of people in Britain.

It is forty-five miles to London as the cock crows.

Most Australians like to live near the sea because it is dry.

The sun never sets on the British Empire because the Empire was on the East and the sun always sets on the West.

In cold climates most rain falls as snow.

The capital of Scotland is S.

One of the tribes of South Africa are called Hotipots.

In India the people are divided into castes and outcasts.

Tundra is a large tin fish often mistaken for salmon.

The largest navel centre in France is breast.

Mountains can be quite sloppy in places.

The tributaries of the Nile are called Juveniles.

The World makes a resolution every 24 hours.

Cologne is famous for the odour made there.

The Seaports of Russia are too far inland for trading purposes.

In the United States people are put to death by elocution.

A mountain range was a cooking stove used at high altitudes.

The population was very dense because of the smoke coming from the chimneys.

Herrings go about the sea in shawls.

Volcanoes are due to the infernal heat of the earth.

'Name the five continents.' 'a, e, i, o, u.'

The Red Sea is joined to the Mediterranean by the Sewage Canal.

Chicago is a large town at the bottom of Lake Michigan.

The Hindus and Muslims are very religious people. They will have nothing to do with each other.

My Auntie Jenny went to Venice and had a great time on a gondolier.

Edinburgh New Town is now very old but the Old Town must be older.

My uncle lives in the knighted steaks of America.

A cannibal is two men who kill one another.

In the tribes of South America a girl can be a mother at eight and a granny before she becomes a woman.

A dingo is a bird with the face of a dog.

All French men are alcoholics because they do not drink orange juice and tea like we do.

There is a saying: 'The Englishman eats to live, the Frenchman eats to die.'

The French built the Sacre Coeur Church in memory of a plague sent by the Germans.

You can buy coffee or a bear in French cafes.

'Where are the Urals?' 'In the boys' toilet, sir.'

French cooks spend a long time papering food.

The oldest member of the Commonwealth is 108.

The Zulus live in mud huts and have rough mating on the floor.

A lumberjack is what you cut down trees with.

The savage which is fairly clean is called effluent.

A croft farmer only has what is necessary.

The stuff that comes out of a volcano is malt and larva.

Philadelphia means 'the City of Brotherly Love'.

'What will Britain be free of in the 1990s?' 'Industry, sir?'

Less people are born in developed countries therefore the population has slowed down.

The peopul in developing countries are eliterit.

The place of the film where mountains took part in *The Sound of Music* was Austria.

What is the significance of the continental shelf? It provides good breeding grounds for the fishermen.

Examples of root crops are turnips, swedes and marigolds.

At the geography lesson the teacher asked the class to look at their knives when they went home to see where they were made (expecting Sheffield). Next day one little boy put up his hand and said his knives came from Ferranti.

Eskimoes live in Iceland and rub noses as a greeting probably to keep warm. It is the only part of their body not covered up as they have to breathe.

The Venetians go about in Gladiolas.

Hush puppies pull sledges for Eskimos.

What do the French call the English Channel? It is a kind of perfume.

The Stock Exchange is a place in London where cattle and pigs are bought.

The horizon is a line where the earth and the sky meet, but disappear when you get there.

One of the chief dam places in Egypt is Aswan.

What is meant by the 'Relief of the Land'? If you have been out at sea on a boat and had a rough time, you would say that it is a relief to be back on the land again.

Marseilles is a large town on Frances bottom.

Eskimos hunt seals with hairpins.

A place where towns and cities and lots of people live is called a conor basin.

In the north of Scotland some of the people speak Garlic.

A Fakir is a Hindu twister.

People who live in Italy are called Stallions.

Latitude tells you how cold you are and longtitude how hot you are.

Take Ireland, the country where, if it isn't raining bullets on the politicians, it's raining water on the bogs.

The probable cause of earthquakes may be attributed to bad drainage and neglect of the sewage.

Name the English lakes. Ulleswater, Derwent Water and Bayswater.

The chief bays in the South of England are Torbay, Poole Bay and Bombay.

What are the main feeders of the Amazon? Alligators.

The meridian of Greenwich is a line that isn't there, kept at Greenwich to measure the time with.

Lemons are a quirk of nature. They commit suicide by jumping over cliffs into the sea.

Brussels is famous for its carpets and sprouts.

The Laplander lives by hunting and fishing. If he catches a whale he takes it home to his tent and his wife will cook it for his supper.

In India rats eat 20% of the rice crop. In Brazil they drink 20% of the coffee.

Clearly a budding Scottish Nationalist, one pupil asked to point out where England was on the map said, 'There, Miss, hanging on to the foot of Scotland.'

In Norway there is a town called Hell, although it is really a cold country.

On holiday, we had sum difacutes with the langwig. But my dad new enouf french to get threw.

Eskie Moes live in cold lands because it would be too far for them to travel to get heat.

When I go abrod I like to be in a place where there is see, sand and lots and lots of bitches.

The Legend is the part of the map which may not be true.

The Rhine flows horizontally through Switzerland and then it turns round and flows vertically through Germany.

If I had to live in a foreign country, I suppose I wouldn't mind East Anglia.

In cold weather the Eskimos turn their skins inside out to trap the heat.

Detergent is a special liquid for dissolving Greece

My cousin came to visit us. He is an a stralyin.

In that country they make rubber by cutting the bark off a hyena tree.

To make the buildings in San Francisco safe from earthquakes they are built so that they don't quite touch the ground.

An Edinburgh teacher was talking to her class about the various Celtic languages and referred to the Welsh speakers.
'Now, where in Scotland would you hear a language that you would not be able to understand?' she asked, pointing to the map. Without any hesitation, one pupil shouted out, 'Glasgow, Miss!'

The first time I went on the boat to Ireland, I was very sick. My mother had a birth and she was alright.

'Most people in our neighbourhood like to go on continental holidays,' wrote a pupil. 'Not me! I can see all the sites I want to see here in Britain.'

'If the wind is blowing from the North, which side of the school would you go to get shelter?' 'The inside, Sir.'

Q. Name five animals that inhabit the Polar Regions?
A. Three seals and two polar bears.

Faintly Franglais

Language teachers are used to correcting errors but some of them are redeemed by their unconscious humour:

Very well, my son. *Très puits, mon soleil.*

Ça va bien? Are you going as well?

La Propriete c'est le Vol. Private Ownership is Theft.

L'Anglais avec son sang-froid habituel.
The Englishman had his usual bloody cold.

Est-il parti, ma tante? Is there a party, My aunt?

La raison du plus fort est toujours la meilleure. The biggest raisins are the best.

La pauvre femme turna vers . . . The poor woman turned green . . .

Prenez garde que votre cheval ne prenne pas le mors entre les dents.
Take care that your horse doesn't die of toothache.

J'ai hâté de l'embrasser. I hated to embrace her.

Elle me conta son cas. She counted me her cash.

Je frappe, la sentinelle ouvre. I knocked the sentinel over.

L'encre est sèche. The uncle is dry.

Un espagnol de forte taille. A spaniel with forty tails.

Il m'a tant frappé. He struck my aunt.

Un grand garçon à lunettes. A big lunatic boy.

Il avait un couteau à la main. He made a curtsy to the sink.

L'usine était située dans un quartier désèrt.
A quarter of the factory was deserted.

J'ai grand faim. I have a big wife.

Dieu et mon droit. My God you're right!

Le garçon avait trois ans. The boy had three asses.

Joie de vivre. Whisky.

Tout à fait. He had everything made.

Emporté par la colère. Carried off by the collar.

Tâtez cette étoffe: elle est mince. Taste this stuff: it's mince.

La bougie: The mouth you speak through.

Le chef de gare: The chief cook.

Au bord de la mer: All aboard the train.

One of the famous sights in Paris is the Sacred Cow (*Sacre Coeur*).

Beurre – cold.

Les Peupliers minces frissonnaient dans la forêt.
The people were frying mince in the forest.

Je résus à son adresse un coup d'épée dans la poitrine.
I received in his house a letter in poetry.

Montrez moi le chemin qui conduit à la ville.
Show me the shirts that were made in the town.

C'est égal. Dès qu'ils furent loin, je sortie de ma cachette.
All the same, as furious as a lion, I took out my hatchet.

Oublier les glaces de son age.
Because of his age he was obliged to wear glasses.

Une grande foule attirée par les spectacles.
A crowd of people wearing spectacles.

Parchemin. A side road.

Heureusement, il est parti. It was a hilarious party.

Il est défendu de fumer. He is trying to defend his smoking.

Dépêchez-vous! Would you like some peaches?

Qui habitaient dans la grande maison blanche?
Who whitewashed the big house?

Histoire de s'amuser. History made him laugh.

Je suis très heureux de faire votre connaissance.
I am very pleased to be connected with you.

Un filet mince de fumée. A fillet of smoked mince.

C'est bon à travailler mais ce n'est pas bon de pas le faire.
It is good to travel, but not so good to pay the fare.

Avoirdupois. Have some green peas.

The money was left in his will. *L'argent fut gauché dans sa volonté.*

I had to fly for my life. *J'avais à mouché pour ma vie.*

Au bord de la mer. Aboard with mother.

Cela va sans dire. He walks without talking.

Plus ça change, plus c'est la même chose!
The more change you have the more difficult it is to chose.

Défense d'afficher. No fishing!

Mal de mer. Mother is ill.

Mes memoirs sont peu préçis. My memoirs are precious few.

Un homme d'ésprit. A publican.

Barely Biblical

What is the outward and visible sign or form in the rite of baptism? The baby.

A graven image was what was put in the ground over the bodies of dead people.

What is meant by the verse in the Bible, 'Sufficient unto the day is the evil thereof . . .' It means that you mustn't do too many bad things in the one day.

A parable was a heavenly story with no earthly meaning.

Insects smoked in the church where the worshippers gathered.

I saw the Archbishop at my confirmation service and now I know what a crook looks like.

The man fell by the roadside but everyone walked past him except the good Sam Marathon.

It seems the Parable of the Sower can be confusing to some: . . . and some seed fell on stony ground and the fowls of the air sprang up and choked them.

Q. Who built the Ark?
A. Joan.

The spies said that the Promised Land was a land 'flowing with milk and honey' and they brought back a bunch of grapes to prove it.

'Mummy, I heard that Jesus' father painted cars.' 'No dear, he was a joiner. What made you think that?' 'Well, the teacher said he was a car painter.'

Joseph lived a very straight life so Pharaoh made him a great ruler.

Faith. That quality which enables us to believe that which we know to be untrue.

The class had been told the story of Abraham and Isaac, emphasising that God was testing Abraham's faith when he commanded him to sacrifice his son on the altar. Asked later to write about the dramatic incident using their own words, one fellow wrote, ' . . . there was I, bound hand and foot, stretched out on the altar. My father had a big knife in his hand and held it over me ready to plunge it into my stomach, when a big voice said, 'Abraham! Stop! You've passed your test.'

Samson was caught by the Philippines.

In a prize essay competition sponsored by the local church a child was writing about the story of Samuel on the subject 'How God talks to us.' Samuel's mother Hannah is speaking: 'If you give me a son, God, I'll give him back to you.' God replies: 'O.K. Hannah, it's a deal.'

When the minister visited the school he spoke to a quiet little lad at the front but could get nothing out of him. He was unaware that he was new to the class that morning. Later he tried to ask him a few questions to involve him. 'Tell me son, what do you know about Jesus?' When he got no reply, the boy next to him piped up, 'Please minister, he doesn't know anything about Jesus, he only came from Glasgow yesterday.'

Hymns and psalms are favourites for misquotation:

'He's got your wee brother in his hands.'
(He's got you and me brother in his hands.)

'In past George Green he leadeth me.'
(In pastures green he leadeth me.)

'We can sing though full we be.'
(Weak and sinful though we be.)

'A wean in a manger.' (Away in a manger.)

The school chaplain was talking to a group of infants about 'peace'.
'Who was the greatest peacemaker? he asked. 'Jesus,' said a little girl.
'Yes, good, why?'
'Well, he made 5000 "pieces" for the crowd of people who were hungry.'

The teacher was a little confused when the little girl insisted that Mary and Joseph must have been freezing cold with no clothes on in the stable. The matter was cleared up when she read the line of the carol she had been teaching. Mary and Joseph in stable bare . . .'

The infant teacher was amused when a little girl in her class said that the ark landed on Mount Anorak.

The infant class was asked to draw a picture of Mary and Joseph with the baby Jesus in the flight into Egypt. One little boy had a super drawing and the delightful finishing touch was a little suitcase on the donkey's back with 'J.C.' on it.

The teacher was telling the infant class about the birth of Jesus and had reached the point when the wise men appeared to visit the new born Baby. 'And what do you think Mary would have said to the men?' she asked the class. One little voice piped up, 'My Mummy would have said, "What time of night is this to visit a baby?" '

Having explained the meaning of BC to her class, the teacher asked for suggestions as to the meaning of AD, and she got the reply, 'After the Devil.'

A mother noticed that her child was practising writing the letter 'I' and she paused between each letter in the row. Curious, she asked the child what she was doing. The little girl replied, 'Well, the teacher read from the Bible today and said that God said, "Draw an I unto me and I will draw an I unto you." '

When saying his prayers at night the boy was heard to say, 'Please God make Paris the capital of Turkey.' When he repeated it several times he was asked by his mother why such a thing was so important. He replied, 'Because that's what I wrote in my Geography exam.'

In reply to a question on the Ten Commandments, 'Was it lawful to buy or sell on the Sabbath Day?' One child replied, 'Buy'.

When asked about animals in the Bible, playing an important part in the life of God's servants, one pupil referred to Balaam's ass who rebuked the man and later on referred to the whale which swallowed Jonah, saying to him, 'Almost thou persuadest me to be a Christian.'

The teacher was involved in explaining about angels and seraphs when one child asked if they flew. 'Yes,' said the teacher, 'it says so in the Bible.' 'I'd like to be one,' said one scruffy little lad who was always in trouble. 'That would be nice,' she smiled. '. . . and I could chase the crows, miss,' he continued.

The teacher was fascinated by the pupil's drawing of the Christmas Story. She had drawn a lot of people and a baby in an aeroplane! 'Please miss, that's the flight into Egypt and Pontius the Pilot.'

This was written in an R.E. exam: 'Christ cured Peter's wife's mother, when she was sick of a fever, and Peter cursed and swore and went out and wept bitterly.'

A class was asked to recite the Creed. One boy stood up and said, 'I believe in God Almighty.' Then the teacher asked another boy to say his bit. He stood up and said, 'I believe in Jesus Christ our Lord.' Then there was a silence. Suddenly a boy at the back said, 'Please sir, the boy who believes in the Holy Spirit is off today.'

Here are some miscellaneous statements, mostly from written work:

A worshipper of Mammon is a bigamist.

Eastern shepherds were called Easter shepherds because they were on the hills at Easter and they let their sheep gaze in the fields.

The Canaanites were chapel and the Israelites were church.

As this was a holy day, the priest washed the beggars' feet and gave arms to the poor.

Jeremiah gave his people a massage.

Paraphrase the following: 'God so loved the world . . . that whosoever believeth in him should not perish . . .' This means that all who believe in God's son would not freeze but have a long life.

Our Father, who art in Heaven, Harold be Thy name.

Ambiguity is telling the truth when you don't want to.

'Follow me and I will make you vicious old men.'

'Surely good Mrs Murphy shall follow me all the days of my life.'

Medieval Church Law stated that an Authorised Virgin should be chained to every pulpit for the sole use of the clergy.

Thou shalt not admit adultery.

Christians are only allowed one wife. This is called monotony.

Jesus helped leopards to get rid of their spots.

The man asked Jesus what he could do to inherit internal life.

Guinnessis is the first book of the Bible, Revolutions is the last.

David killed Goliath with the Axe of the Apostles.

The shepherds washed their socks by night.

Liberty of conscience is doing wrong and not worrying about it afterwards.

An unclean spirit is another name for a dirty devil.

Lot's wife looked round and turned a somersault.

Jesus said that we should lay up trousers in heaven for ourselves.

At the end of the church service the child remarked that they 'had sung the dogs holiday and come home.'

Joseph's family flew into Egypt because there was a feminine in their own land.

A graven image in the Bible is an idle maid with hands.

Who wrote the Bible? Wm. Collins & Sons Ltd.

I don't believe in the Devil. It's like Santa Claus, it's your dad all the time.

In a Free Church they read from a book called *The Beverages*.

At the Passover the Jews ate level bread.

The widow's mite was a wee girl healed by Jesus.

Esau was a hairy man in the Bible who wrote fables and sold his copyright for a mess of potash.

What is the chief end of man? His feet.

The teacher was telling her class the Nativity story and was illustrating it with a picture of Mary, Joseph, the Baby Jesus in the manger, flanked by the wise men and the shepherds. She pointed out that poor Mary and Joseph had to spend the night in a stable when Jesus was born. A wee lad piped up: 'Please Miss, they weren't so poor when they got their photos taken!'

When Jesus said, 'No man can have two masters,' he meant that a man should only have one wife.

Moses sent ten plagues to Egypt, the last of them, and the worst, was children.

I like the story about the wee boy who stole the priest's watch. (From the hymn, 'The old man meek and mild, the priest of Israel slept: his watch, the temple child, the little Levite kept.')

Jesus taught a thick crowd a parable.

Please Miss, who cut the grass in the Garden of Eden after Adam was put out?

John Knox was a Protestant and the Church put him in prison for worshipping God.

Day after day the Hebrew women had children in Egypt.

Hannah went to the temple and prayed for a baby. The very next day she had Samuel.

The pulpit is where the vicar perches every Sunday.

They washed their feet in Jesus' time because they might have stood on something nasty on the way.

If Adam and Eve hadn't eaten those apples in the Garden of Eden, we probably wouldn't have to wear any clothes today.

People who are immortal can have the time of their lives.

After doing a project on Holland the teacher was more than a little amused to read one child's R.E. notes: 'Edam and Eve lived in the Garden of Eden.'

Jesus had lots of trouble with the Fairysees.

I wonder if Noah allowed a pair of woodworms into the ark?

A strict Scottish father reprimanded his children for playing at soldiers on the Sabbath. 'But, Dad, we're in the Salvation Army!'

The infants were rehearsing the Nativity Play for the school Christmas concert. The little girl who was Mary, came up to the teacher and gave a big sigh. 'What's wrong dear?' she asked.
'Oh, Mrs Thomson, it's awfully hard work being a virgin.'

If a moslem is allowed more than one wife, how do they all get into a double bed?

It was perhaps nearer to the point when one child wrote, 'Pontius Pilot washed his hands because he had blood all over them.'

What are priests called when they decide not to marry? Bachelors of Divinity.

A pupil who attended a non-denominational school learned that, if he had a note from his parents indicating that he was a Catholic, he need not come to classes until 9.30 am. once a week when the usual R.E. lesson was being given. After writing a note for himself he attended late each Thursday morning. The teacher's suspicions were aroused when he discovered that the fellow didn't attend classes organised for Catholic pupils either.
'You said that you were a Catholic, Danny,' challenged the teacher.
'Yes, Sir, but that was only on Thursdays.'

In India they throw people into the River Ganges so that they will go to heaven more quickly.

We were told that man's chief end was to glorify God and enjoy himself for ever.

I suppose the expression 'spoil the rod' must have meant that you had to give up fishing.

Who was very unhappy when the Prodigal Son returned to his father?
The fatted calf.

The people had lots of problems in these days with the Pharisees and the Seducers.

Abraham nearly sacrificed his son Isaac because he had done a trick on Abraham and he didn't find it funny.

The rich man in the parable was called a fool because it would take him much more time to build a bigger barn and by that time all the crops would be dead.

A vicar wears a dress, wanders around with a big cross round his neck and is usually bald and smiling. He never goes out at night.

On Christmas Day the minister was going round the pews talking to the children. One little girl said, 'If you hear a wee noise and smell a wee smell, Mr Jones, it's only me.' She explained further, 'I got a watch and a bottle of perfume for my Christmas.'

On hearing the story about the Feeding of the Five Thousand, when the disciples collected twelve baskets full of leftovers, one little girl piped up, 'My goodness, I hope Jesus put it in the freezer for another day!'

A bishop wears a metre on his head.

Paul escaped over the walls of Damascus in a bucket.

The Facts of Life

In 1956 the Swedish Education Minister said that sex was compulsory for all school children.

The pancreas is the gland that gives you sexual desire.

Dad wanted to break the news of the addition to the family to his ten-year-old daughter but did not get around to saying anything until the child was born. 'Diane, the fairies have just brought you a baby brother.' 'Lovely,' the girl replied excitedly, 'I must write to John.' Her father was curious to know what she had written to her elder brother who was away from home so he peeped at the letter when she was out. 'Dear John, I told you they had done it. It's come off at last and it's a boy . . . You win!'

Twins are two things which come unexpectedly together.

Twins are two children with the same hair and the same clothes.

'Mummy, where did I come from?' the little girl asked one day on returning home from school. Taking this as a golden opportunity the young mother proceeded to explain the facts of life to her daughter. After some time, and some strange faces from the little girl, she piped up. 'Thanks Mummy, I wanted to know because there's a new girl in our class and she says that she comes from Edinburgh.'

Mummy isn't well today, she's having her pyramid.

The teacher was doing a lesson on human reproduction. After going through it all in great detail she started to recap and asked a girl in the front row: 'The woman produces a seed from her ovaries and the man produces a sperm from his . . . ?' 'Underies, Miss?'

Written in a News Book: 'We were going to have a baby some time but not now. Daddy told me where it is and Mummy has swallowed it.'

Boys and girls develop in different places.

It is difficult to tell the sex of my rabbits, but they know, because Billy and Sammy had little ones last week.

'I know where babies come from, Miss, but if I told you, you wouldn't believe me.'

When a young girl reaches puberty she starts to have a monthly period and develops breasts, but fortunately these only last for five or six days.

When you want to make a baby you need a sperm from the father and an egg from the mother, but it is not always easy to get them together at the right time of the year.

The difference between external and internal fertilisation is that some animals mate inside and some do it in the open air.

The teacher had been pregnant for some time but none of the pupils in her infant class seemed to have noticed her steady growth until one day the dental hygienist called to talk to them about teeth and explained that sweets and chocolates were not only bad for teeth but made you fat, if you ate too many. On returning to the classroom one little lad walked up to the teacher and said, pointing to her tummy, 'I know what you've been doing miss!'

As a gentle introduction to sex education, a teacher decided to talk about the life cycle of the frog. They visited a local pond and one of the children noticed a male frog on the back of a female frog. The pupils were curious to know what was happening so the teacher explained. On hearing this, one little girl, in a rather loud whisper, exclaimed, 'I'll tell you one thing. There's no way my mummy would let my daddy jump on her back like that!'

For Family Planning couples can use all sorts of different forms of contraptions.

Some infants were playing at 'Mums and Dads' in the Wendy House. The teacher's ears pricked up when she heard the following: 'Push! Push! And watch out for the baby!' When the teacher looked in to see what was being acted out, she was amused, and not a little relieved, to discover that a little girl was directing her 'husband' to move the cooker for her.

A kiss is better when the lips are coming together than after.

An eight-year-old came home from school one day and announced to his mum that they had learned all about where babies come from. Interested to know how much he had been told, she asked him to tell her all about it. He was just finishing the rather long and detailed account, when his father arrived home. 'Tell dad all about it too Roger,' said mum. With an exasperated look, he exclaimed, 'Why? Does he not know either?'

When one of her pupils announced that her mummy had just had a baby, the teacher remarked, 'How nice, Susan! Is it a boy or a girl' 'No, not yet, it's just a baby,' she replied.

The following examples were sent in to Grampian Television in response to their request for children's work after discussion of the programme 'Living and Growing'.

When you are small you don't need to worry about all these things, like sex etc.

A lot of people find sex something to laugh at but there is nothing funny about it. I bet even our parents found it funny when they were at school.

If nobody wanted babies there would be nobody left in the world.

When I saw the programme I was taught the most unlikely things.

The programme told us that every lady has a volvo.

I thought the programme was quite educational because if you met someone and you did not know what to do, you could always refer to the programme.

The programme explained how an egg is released from the ovary and does a twenty-eight day cycle along the Fallopian tube.

The sixth programme was about having the baby with names like labourer because it was hard work and looked it too.

Labour can start at any time. It is advisable to have a bag ready.

When the woman is nearly ready to give birth she starts to get contraptions.

. . . then they cut the biblical cord.

Next the midwife will take the baby in her arms and juggle the baby.

The difficulty which children have in appreciating adult imagery is highlighted in the following humorous but sobering account of one child's misunderstanding of advertising about AIDS.
The class was discussing Cold Lands and icebergs were mentioned. One boy said, 'Sir, you can catch AIDS from icebergs, can't you?'
Realising that the boy was quite serious, the teacher asked him why he thought that and learned that the fellow had seen a warning leaflet with the caption, 'AIDS, it's only the tip of the iceberg.'

The difference between a bee and a wasp is that a bee has a round end and a wasp has a sharp end.

Teachers nowadays are very aware that they must be careful when talking about mummies and daddies as there are so many one parent families. The fact was brought home to one teacher when observing children at play one day. 'If you don't behave yourself, I'll get a divorce and live with my other boyfriend!' announced one little girl to a little boy who wouldn't be bossed around by her.

When visiting a farm with his class, the city child was fascinated to see milk being taken from a cow. Later on they were given milk to drink and scones with honey. 'Mmm, honey. Do you keep a bee as well?' he asked intelligently.

'Mum, where were you and dad on the 15th September, 1975,' asked the ten-year-old, out of the blue, after sitting at the table for some time with a pencil and paper.
'How should I know?' asked mum, standing at the ironing table. 'Why are you asking anyway?'
'Well we've been doing 'Living and Growing' at school and they explained how long it takes for a baby to grow. And I was working out my birthday and . . .' 'Look, don't bother me just now, ask your father.' came the evasive interruption.

Through the Microscope

Respiration is caused by wearing a heavy sweater on a hot day.

Plants are different from animals because they do not go to the toilet.

Plankton is a very heavy type of wood.

A membrane is a brain with a very long memory.

The light passes through the lens and is focused on the rectum.

Yeast is the protection inside a cow around its liver.

An amoeba is a small orgasm you usually get in water.

To treat a patient for shock, rape him in a warm blanket.

Mushrooms always grow in damp places so they look like umbrellas.

Monkeys eat bananas as well as human beings.

The alimentary canal runs from your mouth to the rectory.

Comatose – dead feet, like when you get frostbite.

Snails have to slide along and hope for the best.

An octopus is a flat sort of fish with eight testacles.

The purpose of the black cloth over the belljar is to stop the plant from being distracted.

Hair is sort of threads coming out of your head; they grow just like they was living.

Get a peanut, weigh it, burn it to nothing and then reweigh it.

The spine is a bunch of bones that runs up and down the back and holds the ribs together. The skull sits at one end and I sit at the other.

A hereditary disease is one you can catch from your relatives. Like when my sister got chickenpox, I caught it too.

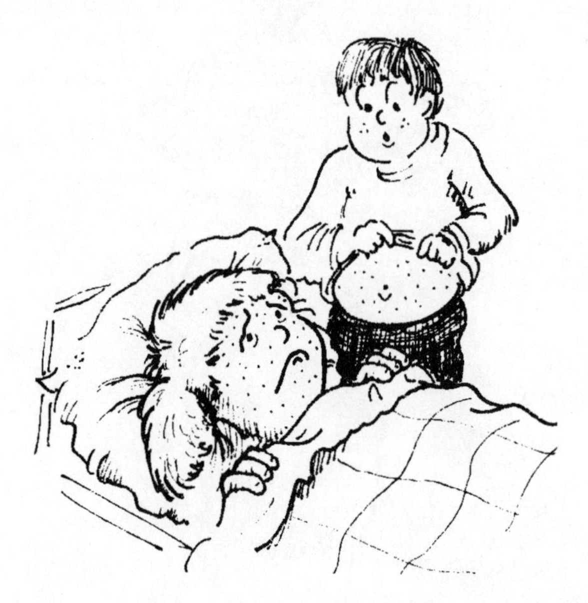

Pins and Pancakes

Interfacing is to stop your arms and neck fraying.

Before you can make a dress you must have a pattern, or if you are very experienced you can cut it out of your head.

Rhubarb is a kind of celery gone bloodshot.

Q: Name two fillings for a duvet.
A: Jam and Cream.

Old people often eat a lot of cheap carbohydrate and can become stricken with illness or obscenity.

A common disease of cereal crops is wheat germ.

One girl wrote the following recipe in her exercise book:

Apple Crumble:
3oz margarine   llb apples
4oz plain flour   2oz sugar
Method: Slice ruhbarb . . . sprinkle sugar over ruhbarb.
Place breadcrumbs on top of ruhbarb.

If you cannot find an onion, take a leak instead.

'Baking blind' means putting something in the oven and not bothering to look at it.

Another way of doing potatoes is to do them with your jacket on.

Liver and kidney are awful (offal).

Egg whites make a souffle blow up. Gelignite makes it set.

Pastas come from Cornwall.

Apple grumble is my favourite pudding.

If you do not take enough of vitamin C you will most likely suffer from vitamin D.

Bass is a beverage made from the fish of the same name.

Why does the grocer sell cured ham? Because he couldn't sell it if it was still ill.

Caviare generally comes from a surgeon.

Experiments have shown that vitamin E makes rats sexy. We don't know about men yet.

To work best in a kitchen, especially in a hotel, it is important for a woman to be absolutely sterile.

Oysters are usually found in beds at the seaside.

What is the best known cereal in Britain? Coronation Street.

In Italy they are very fond of food such as graffitti.

A sherrif is a French cook.

Why not eat Italians for a change. Spaghetty bolagnaged and a glass of good red wine make a nice change.

A la carte means you can have everything that's on the trolley.

When fresh vegetables are not available you can always go and get canned.

Please Miss, I couldn't spell scones so I've put buns instead.

Carbohydrates are fattening. Carbolodrates are not.

Hold the prawn between your fingertips. Straighten it out, then jerk its head and bottom together. The prawn will immediately jump out of its jacket.

If baking powder is not added to the plain flour your scones will not stand and may end up as pancakes.

Gently knead the dough until it is round and flat adding a sprinkle more flour if knead be.

The wine is best chilled and served in a giraffe.

Salt is stuff which, if it is not boiled with potatoes, makes them nasty.

Mostly Musical

Some instruments are: viles, cellars, trumpets, hornets, baboons, old boys and bubble bases.

Rumpelstiltskin was a Nationalist Composer from Russia.

Mozart lived until the end of his life.

Chopin died of constipation (consumption).

Handel's father would not allow him upstairs at night to practice on his spinster (spinnet).

. . . the famous Russian composer Ripsikcornetoff.

An aria is a very slow, laxative piece of music.

Q. What is this note called? o
A. A semi-beaver.

There are three sections in an orchestra – string, brass and woodworm.

Violin strings are made from cat's whiskers.

Pizzicato means to puke.

One of the smallest members of the percussion family is the tangerine.

Q. Where are the Proms held? A. In the left hand.

Contralto is a low form of music which only women sing.

A scale is an exercise for loosening the fingers. There are two types, diatonic and teutonic.

Archipelagos are the high runs in music which only the best people can sing.

Mozart died from salvation.

Two crotchets make a quaker.

An interval in music is a period for refreshment.

An octet is a figure with eight sides.

D.C. means don't clap!

d.c. = dead

I like the song we learned, I think it was a Negro spiritual, 'Take me back to old Virginity.'

Q. How long do you hold a minim for? A. Three seconds.

A theme is the thing that runs down the leg of your trousers.

Cabarets are entertainments where they can't afford a stage.

A crotchet is a table cloth with fancy sewing.

What do you do when you find a note with a dot after it? Stop.

What does legato mean? With a limp.

A pibroch is a Scotsman with wind.

What do we find below a mezzo-soprano? A stool.

Why do you think the composer wrote the work in two flats? He probably stayed with friends at times.

Arty Crafty

After the woodwork teacher had stressed to the class that the glue should be spread thinly on the joint, he asked a boy who appeared to be half asleep, 'What, Smith, should you not do with the glue?' The boy's answer was a sign of the times. 'Sniff it, Sir.'

The art teacher thought he had explained the meaning of 'tone' and 'shade' until one boy wrote that 'tone' is a colour and 'shade' is using an H.B pencil.

Art Teacher: 'Yes, the face is very good Norman, you seem to have mastered the shading of the nose. I'll just paint out that mark on the upper lip for you and it will be fine. Pupil: 'No, no, Sir, leave it! It's supposed to be a bogie.

On a report card from a woodwork teacher:

All the other boys have produced coffee tables or lamp standards, but alas, Jeremy has only been able to produce a small brown stool.

'Please Sir, can I do one colour over another because I want to do the girl's hair dyed?' 'Why not just paint the colour you want it to be?' 'Please Sir, because this might be the first time anybody's ever done a picture of dyed hair.'

My father is an artist but he only draws the dole just now.

Asked what he knew about the Impressionist Period, one pupil replied that it was a time when paintings made a great impression on people.

Michael Angelo painted the cistern of the chapel.

Inspectors at Large

'An inspector came to our school today. At first we thought he was the new janitor, but he asked questions that a janitor wouldn't ask.'

An inspector took a teacher to task for telling her pupils the meaning of words without leading them to discover it for themselves. To illustrate the point he took the lesson and came to the word 'prancing', which nobody knew the meaning of, so he began to walk around the room in a spirited way. 'Now, what am I doing class?' 'Please sir,' came the reply, 'walking in front of the teacher without saying "Excuse me".'

The inspector obtained the response that 'a pilgrim is a man who goes from place to place.' 'But I go from place to place. Am I a pilgrim?' the gentleman asked. 'No no, sir, a pilgrim's a good man.'

After an inspection of a small school the inspector noticed that a boy was busy drawing and when he asked him to let him see it the boy was reluctant, because he had drawn the gentleman. When the teacher went to fetch it, the little lad whispered, 'Please miss, I've put a tail on him and made it into a wee dog.'

A headmaster was irritated by members of the public entering the playground and using the school toilets. He instructed the janitor to lock the door on the next person he saw sneaking in. Within the hour the janitor managed this and handed the headmaster the key. After an hour or so the headmaster unlocked the toilet and released an infuriated Inspector of Schools.

An inspector arrived at a small rural school one forenoon. It was playtime, and as he made for the entrance he was confronted by a small boy who barred his way and said:
'Did you brush your shoes this morning?' 'Yes, I did.'
'Did you wash your face?' 'Yes, I did that too.'
'And did you remember to brush your teeth?' 'Yes, I gave them a good brush.' 'It's just as well,' said the boy. 'The Inspector's coming today.'

On a tour of schools on a remote Scottish island, an Inspector arranged his programme so that the tiny, one-teacher school close to his base was left until last. He arrived there on the Friday morning to a rather chilly reception.

'All week we have watched you driving past our door,' said the teacher, 'and the children have been so disappointed.' 'And do you know,' she continued, 'these poor girls have had clean white socks on every morning!'

When an inspector from the city visited a small country school he described his home town as a place where everything was dull and grimy, there were few birds, there was a lot of smoke and all you could see were chimneys and roof-tops. 'What sort of place do I come from, do you think?' 'Sounds like a prison, sir.'

An Inspector was visiting a school in a deprived district of a town where the kids were a really rough bunch. He decided to start his inspection with a few questions on mental arithmetic and addressed the first one to a boy in the front row. 'Can you tell me what is seven times eight?' The boy immediately responded with 'fifty-six'. 'Not bad,' said the Inspector. 'Not bad?' said the boy, 'What do you mean, it's perfect!'

Every teacher knows that effective follow-up work is essential after an outdoor study; it is often the part which many children least like if it is not done well. This is illustrated by a conversation overheard by an inspector who quietly joined on to the end of a snake of children making their way back to school along the edge of a playing field. 'Look Billy, there's a rabbit!' 'For goodness sake, don't tell the teacher John, or she'll have us writing about it, or drawing it.'

Teachers' Talk

Communicates fluently: *A constant chatterbox.*

An independent learner: *Will not do what he is told.*

Mixes well with other pupils: *Always chasing the girls.*

Could try harder: *A lazy little rascal.*

Will go far: *An absolute con man.*

A born leader: *A real little bossy boots.*

Is good with his hands: *He still can't read a word.*

He cannot wait to leave school: . . . *and neither can we!*

An active class member: *Will not sit still for two minutes.*

Has a facility with numbers: *Will probably excel at bingo.*

Exams have never been a problem with him: *Has never turned up for one yet.*

Has a ready ear for music: *Never takes off his personal stereo.*

A colourful personality: *Her hair is dyed luminous green.*

His artwork has been displayed in every corridor: *We have now confiscated the aerosol.*

Has easily mastered a second language: *Swears like a trooper.*

His work will no doubt improve next year: *It's a pity he leaves school this summer.*

Will go far: *The further away from here the better.*

Communicates fluently: *Talks like a budgie.*

Writes imaginatively: *Particularly good at absence notes.*

A solitary child: *Personal hygiene leaves a lot to be desired.*

Determined child: *Lacks all scruples.*

Very bright, above average pupil: *Thinks he knows more than the teachers.*

He has a winning manner: *Will be good with the pools.*

Satisfactory progress: *I've said that about everyone.*

He is good at sports: *Certainly in for the high jump one of these days.*

Easily distracted: *Never listens to a word I say.*

Very consistent work: *Has failed every exam so far.*

Enjoys outdoor activities: *It would help if he came to school more often.*

Afterflaws

My mother wasn't healthy and she was warned not to have children by her doctor.

He suddenly realized he needed her as he knew nothing about household choirs.

My arm was in a lot of pain so I told a nurse and she passed it on to a doctor.

Very slowly I began to make a rapid recovery.

They was very pleased and I said I would treat them to a slapup meal including my beautiful dog and my best companion Ben.

My sister and her boyfriend canoed all evening on the front room sofa and I wasn't allowed in to watch television.

I think hanging should be brought back, gelatine, the lot.

The best part of the show was the great Alfredo and his performing loins.

On our trip to York we were allowed to see parts of the minister not normally exhibited to the general public.

Sarah knew she was being a bit erotic, but she had a reputation for having a very imaginative imagination.

The expression 'the pain got right into the rib' is unusual as it does not state where the 'rib' is, but the reader can guess. I think he uses it as he knows the reader will have a good idea of where and what it is.

A sixty-foot tree can break wind for up to 200 yards.

He sighed a heave of relief.

Why do I always get the blame? Why do you always make me the skateboard?

I was passing water over a bridge, when suddenly I noticed the sleepy village in the distance.

'Muttonchop whiskers' are those wee bits of hair that you get on chops from the butchers.

She was good at everything she done in school. She won the duck's award for three years.

A refugee keeps order at a football match.

If a lady should faint in church put her head between the legs of the nearest medical man.

A grass widow is the wife of a dead vegetarian.

What is a herbaceous border? One who boards all week and goes home on Saturdays and Sundays.

The jockey lost two of his teeth when the horse fell and had to be destroyed.

Dust is mud with the juice squeezed out.

Snoring is letting off sleep.

A hostage is a lady who entertains visitors.

Tarzan is a short name for the American flag. Its full name is Tarzan Stripes.

It is dangerous to walk there at nights. I might be murdered and have to go without my tea.

Looking for the word 'wedge', the teacher asked the class, 'what small thing could I use to keep the door open?' The amusing response from one pupil was 'You could get a wee boy from the infant room.'

What did the man mean when he said 'Time will tell'? He meant that he would phone the speaking clock.

An autobiography is a book about cars.

When he says he executed his business there, it is just another way of saying he gave it the chop.

If all education were abolished in the world today the effects would be felt in the world to come.

Things bundled together are called a cloister.

Explain the meaning of 'What he said was sharp and to the point.' It means that he was very blunt when he spoke.

Daddy hasn't managed to give up smoking completely, but he has cut it down by a hundred per cent.

The teacher explained that herbivorous meant eating plants and carnivorous meant eating flesh. 'What would you call an animal that eats everything?' he asked. 'A greedy glutton' was the apt response.

At the Coronation they could not use the Queen for practising so they used a real lady instead.

A pupil was asked to stand up and give a sentence with the word 'canal' in it. He offered 'At 3.30pm when the bell goes we canal go home.'

Three shots rang out. Two men fell dead and the other went through his hat.

Complete the following, Susan: 'It takes two to make . . .' (Looking for the answer 'a quarrel') 'Love,' was the coy suggestion.

An avenue is really just another name for a road but there are no council houses on them.

'Untapped potential' means being able to have a telephone conversation without anyone listening in.

Correct the following: a) The hen has three legs. b) Who done it? One small boy seeing some connection between the two answered: 'The hen never done it, God done it.'

When pheasants are sold you have to buy them in braces.

Anxious that the boys should behave themselves when they went to their grandparents for a short stay, they were coaxed to be on their best behaviour. However, the young one said, 'What will we get if we are good?' The older boy was quite shocked. 'That's terrible Michael, you should be like me and be good for nothing.'

It is very important in Britain to show your birth certificate to prove that you have been born.

'We have three cats and one is a tom, but we are getting him dressed,' explained the child to the teacher. 'Fancy putting clothes on a cat,' a voice exclaimed from the back of the room.

The bride carried a bunch of flowers on her weeding day.

Prices tend to flatuate quite often.

Moths don't eat much. They just eat holes.

When you stroke a cat by drawing your hand along its back, it cocks up its tail like a ruler so you can't get any further.